THE SILENCE OF GOD

OTHER BOOKS BY JAMES P. CARSE

Breakfast at the Victory: The Mysticism of Ordinary Experience
Finite and Infinite Games

James P. Carse

THE
SILENCE
OF GOD

Meditations on Prayer

HarperSanFrancisco
A Division of HarperCollinsPublishers

FIRST HARPERCOLLINS PAPERBACK EDITION PUBLISHED IN 1995

Library of Congress Cataloging-in-Publication Data:
Carse, James P.
The silence of God : meditations on prayer / James P.
Carse—1st HarperCollins paperback ed.
    p.   cm.
Originally published: New York : Macmillan © 1985.
  ISBN 0–06–061410–2 (pbk. : alk. paper)
1. Prayer—Christianity—Meditations. I. Title.
[BV210.2.C356   1995]
248.3'2—dc20   95–10094
                                                   CIP

95 96 97 98 99 RRD(H) 10 9 8 7 6 5 4 3 2 1

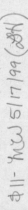

To the memory of Louise Constance Keene

Contents

Contents

Preface

Prayer may be the most universally shared feature among the world's religions. Krishna, Maitreya Buddha, and the Virgin Mary have almost nothing in common, but all three are regularly prayed to by their worshipers.

Prayers can be silent, chanted, written, memorized, extemporaneous, spoken in tongues, sung, ritually scheduled, ceremonial, composed for special liturgical occasions. They can be uttered in praise, shame, sorrow, or despair. But for all these differences, the essential character of prayer remains the same: It is speech addressed to the Divine or to divine powers.

There is obviously something about prayer that accounts for its persistent vitality across the religious traditions. Yet, remarkably, little has been written about the nature of prayer itself, while much has been said about the value of prayer and about the content and discipline of prayer. There is even considerable literature on religious language, or what philosophers like to call "god-talk," talking *about* God. In all this, however, talking *to* God remains a largely unexplored phenomenon.

This book began with a request from a group of laity and nonacademic friends to facilitate a discussion of what prayer is. I agreed to do so not because this was something I already knew, but because it was my question as well. It is still my question. These meditations respond to a vacuum, they don't fill it. And the lively response to the book's initial publication ten years ago indicates that this is a question for many others as well. I am pleased to think its re-publication may stimulate a still wider inquiry into the nature of prayer.

James P. Carse
January 1995

THE SILENCE OF GOD

"Ask and you shall receive."

My earliest memory of anything religious is being carefully instructed by my grandmother in the proper method of prayer. She was in the habit of taking me each Sunday to her neighborhood Methodist church, keeping me at her side through the entire service, mercifully shielding me from the routine of Sunday School where unluckier children were confined to the tasks of coloring Joseph's robe or making a miniature church of used popsicle sticks. Because it was built in the semicircular shape popular among Methodists, the sanctuary was enclosed within a 180° arc of translucent windows that bathed the entire proceeding in warm yellow light. The sermons were doubtless adequate by the standards of Ohio Methodism, but I remember nothing of them. I do remember how I got patted and stroked by a lot of other children's grandparents, and how my grandmother was complimented on my behavior in church. But what I remember best is putting my hand into hers during the prayers and trying to squeeze my eyes shut the way she did.

It was the practice of shutting my eyes that was certainly the most impressive feature of praying for me. My grandmother insisted so firmly on it that I tried to keep out even the yellow light. But the practice mystified me. The only other reasons I knew for intentionally shutting your eyes were to pretend that you were asleep when someone looked in at night, or to pretend that you were someone else and somewhere else. Now I was to pretend that I was talking to someone I could not see and could not know.

"Always remember," my grandmother would explain, "though nobody can see God, he can see you. He knows everything in your heart. So, whenever you speak to him, speak from your heart."

But I was a little boy, and hardly even knew I had a heart. Besides, everyone could already see me, and I did not pray to them. Apparently you only pray to someone who remains hidden, like talking on a telephone to someone who never says anything back.

Nearly fifty years later this weightless dab of Methodist piety has become an awesome challenge. Speak to God from your heart. I am no longer a little boy, and have learned in becoming an adult another way of shutting my eyes: inwardly, against my heart. It is no longer a matter of not seeing God as it is not seeing myself. The problem is not pretending to speak to someone I cannot know, but speaking as someone I know I am not.

I am now persuaded that speaking to God from your heart is the only real religious issue there is. Learn to pray, and all else follows. It is not the *content* of the heart that matters, only the ability to speak from it. We sometimes think that a heart full of hatred, or envy, or a heart drained of passion, disqualifies itself for authentic prayer. The task, however, is not preparing your heart for prayer, but speaking from your heart as it is. We can easily get this backward in the religious life, assuming that our primary spiritual assignment is to make ourselves presentable to God instead of presenting ourselves to God as we are.

This book is a series of meditations on the challenge of speaking to God from the heart. They were originally prepared for a group of friends with whom the discussion of these issues has been fundamental to my understanding of them. By putting them onto paper I only intend to extend the circle of friends with whom these crucial spiritual issues may be explored. By no means do I present myself as a master of the religious life; I am but one member of a journeying community who depend on one another for a renewal of spirit and mind in our continuing quest for spiritual wholeness.

Because the subject of prayer is so elemental to the religious life, the conceptual tools for these meditations are very simple. I shall rely on an observed distinction, and an experienced fact.

The *observed distinction*: Religious language falls roughly into two categories: that which is said *about something*, and that which is said *to someone*. I shall refer to these categories as theology and prayer. There are many forms of each, and varied styles, but neither loses its character of being about something or to someone.

Of course, it is possible to categorize all language under the same terms. We often speak about something, and it seems that we are almost always speaking to someone. A question of boundaries arises here. When do we cross the line into theology when we are speaking about something, and prayer when we are speaking to someone? Theology is usually marked off by the verbal content of what is being said. Some persons argue, for example, that genuine theology must be closely tied to scripture. Indeed, some persons go so far as to say that scripture *is* theology, and all the theology we need. This view appears in the claim that scripture is truth itself; that is it is indisputably true information *about something*. On the other hand, it has become fashionable recently to consider theoretical physics as a form of theology. It seems to be about the same topics that theological discourse is about: the origin and destiny of the universe, the statistical improbabilities of the appearance of life, the immaterial nature of matter, and so forth.

The boundaries for prayer are also ambiguous. Of course, we could say simply enough that anything said to God is prayer. But if you wonder, as I did when I was a little boy, how you can find a proper object to aim your words at with your eyes closed, the question of defining prayer becomes more difficult. How can you know that it is truly to God that you are speaking? There is a theological method of defining prayer. One might, for example, develop an image of God from scripture, then pray to such a being. Indeed, one might even assume that a primary task for theologians is to provide an understanding of God that makes it possible for us to know whom we are addressing in our prayers.

But to use theology to make prayer possible is getting it backward again. Prayer which depends on theology to define its proper addressee is bound to be theological prayer—that is, discourse about something and not to someone. How often we hear prayers that sound like sermons; how often we hear ourselves praying in a way that seems to be informing or instructing God instead of speaking to God from our hearts.

I should rather consider prayer to be genuine depending on its origin, and not on its object or its content. What is truly spoken from the heart is prayer. Does it not matter then *to whom* one speaks? Will anyone, or anything, do as the addressee? The answer to this question is elusively simple: *Speak from your heart and you will speak to God.*

The substance of much that is to come in these pages is meant to elucidate this point, but I can anticipate it here by several brief observations. The meaning of the verb, to pray, is to ask, or even to beg. The heart is a beggar. Petition and supplication are its natural modes. As I shall try to make clear later, we live by asking; we have nothing we do not ask for. What is more, there is a kind of wisdom in begging. We know that we cannot beg pennies of the penniless, and we do not ask fools for guidance. But then neither do we ask anything of the rich or wise if we believe ourselves sufficient in wealth or understanding. Begging comes from need. Only the poor can be beggars whether their poverty be in goods or spirit. If you know your need, if you do not shut your eyes to the truest longing of your heart, you will know where to take your petitions.

It is not theology or philosophy, but only your heart, that will lead you to God.

The text for these meditations is Jesus' declaration, "Ask and you shall receive." What is implied in this remarkable teaching is that there is a great spiritual abundance, an unlimited treasure, available to those who ask. The issue here is not talking God into something; it is not finding ways of influencing the Almighty. The issue is simpler by far. Just ask. All else follows. Jesus does not say, Ask and you will get what you deserve, or were clever enough to think of, or were lucky enough to be given. By putting the *and* between asking and receiving they become part of the same movement. There is no asking without receiving and no receiving without asking.

There are many questions raised about the *efficacy* of prayer. Are prayers really answered? How is it possible that we could persuade God to give us what we want? Does God not already know what we want anyway? Besides, what sort of a God do we have whose will we can influence through our requests? And so on. But these questions are all theological. They are an attempt to get everything in order before we begin. For that reason they fail if they succeed. If we have an understanding of these matters, it is an understanding *about* God, with the result that we will pray about something and not to someone. What we ask for will be determined by our understanding and not our hearts. Questions such as these will therefore be ignored in these meditations.

By the way, if you read into these remarks a strong antitheological bias on my part, I demur. My only objection here is to the claimed *primacy* of theology. While it is true that theology cannot lead us to prayer, it is still the case that prayer can lead us to theology. You may reply, Yes, but to a theology that has nothing to do with the truth, since it is not about anything verifiable, or even testable, and therefore a theology about which one could hardly be serious. To that I can only agree; but I agree happily, for this raises theology from science to art. This means that theology is no longer a region where we engage each other in dispute, attempting to mark out the boundaries for proper belief, but where we come together in creativity and imagination, unwilling to put any boundaries around the truth. Theology is inevitable, like spirited conversation between friends who have much to share with each other. It is only when theology is directed at opponents with whom we share nothing, and want to share nothing, that it falsely asserts its primacy. Those who can pray with each other will take up theology with a natural enthusiasm that makes it a joyous discipline.

This, then, is the first conceptual tool: a distinction between theology and prayer, or speaking about something and speaking to someone.

The second conceptual tool is the *experienced fact*: in all candor I must say that I have never heard God speak, nor can I even say that I have ever read what I know God to have said. What I have experienced, and experienced repeatedly, is the silence of God.

For many years the silence of God was a distressing matter to me. Indeed, I did not consider it an experience at all, but the absence of an experience. It was because God said nothing that I assumed I had had no significant religious experience. The reason for my distress, quite frankly, was that I wanted some sort of certainty on which I could rest my religious beliefs. As it was I had a few tired proofs for the existence of God and the general worth of religion, but I did not really believe them myself. So I wanted genuine proof, even if it was an inner disclosure, a private communication, something more exciting and more convincing than the yellow light and the loving grandparents in the neighborhood church of my childhood. But over a considerable period of time I came increasingly to see that the silence of God is not the absence of an experience but is the very essence of religious experience.

In coming to realize the positive religious value of the silence of God I passed through a number of discouraging, nonproductive, dead-end exercises in my spiritual life; nothing so remarkable as the mystics' gloomy cloud of unknowing or the dark night of the soul, but instructive nonetheless. One moment is worth recalling here. The silence of God was most troubling to me during my college years when I sometimes went to the extreme of walking about on isolated country roads at night, demanding that God manifest himself. Only once did anything surprising occur. Coming into my dormitory room very late one night, long after my roommates had gone to sleep, I threw myself fully clothed on the bed. Several hours later a powerful voice woke me out of a dreamless sleep. I had the clear impression that someone had spoken directly into my ear, and had spoken with such terrifying authority that I sprang onto the floor. It took me a few seconds to make sure I had heard the words correctly. Yes, there was no doubt about it. What the voice had said was, RISE AND MAKE YOUR BED! I looked around the room in the faint morning light to see whether anyone else had been awakened by this command, or whether someone had played a trick on me. All three of my roommates slept on undisturbed.

Rise and make your bed? My bed *was* made. I never even pulled back the blankets. What did it all mean? By the middle of the next day I had convinced myself that the voice was most certainly of divine origin, partly because it seemed so clearly to have come from without, and partly because it possessed such compelling authority. I also decided that the mysterious message was not at all frivolous as it seemed, but was to be interpreted as a code for something far more portentous. It seemed exactly the sort of proof I had longed for; but the more I thought about it the less I was sure what it proved. For that reason I told no one about it. I could not imagine how I could report it without sounding ridiculous. It was years before I did tell anyone, but by then I could see myself that it was ridiculous. I had found that every interpretation I tried to put on the words was sillier than the last. Rise and make my bed? Some basis for faith.

Speaking now theologically, that is to say whimsically, I can well imagine that someone did play a trick on me. I can visualize an angelic presence musing, "If that arrogant young man asks for one more divine revelation, let us give him one." Like the Buddha who would give ridiculous answers to his disciples' metaphysical questions (such as, Does the soul exist after death?) my angel gave me a message that refused to be a message. It was a way of showing me that I was trying to back into faith by means of theology. All I wanted God to do was to provide me with just one indisputable theological item so I could avoid the embarrassment of standing there with nothing but a longing heart. God did not cooperate.

This incident, however, was not in itself decisive. In retrospect it is more revealing than I thought at the time, but that is largely because I have come to learn that the silence of God is acknowledged in a variety of ways in many spiritual traditions. The essential insight here is that in an encounter with divine reality we do not hear a voice but acquire a voice; and the voice we acquire is our own. It is an experience in which we find we say what we never thought it was possible to say.

Because this insight is fundamental to the problem of prayer, and because the notion of the silence of God is no doubt still puzzling to the reader, the first meditation will explore the deeper meaning of this silence.

The following three meditations deal with the inherent structure of prayer: what we can truly ask God for, what God can actually give us, and what we are able in fact to receive from God.

The Present Silence of God as the Silent Presence of God

"The Tao that can be spoken is not the eternal Tao." These are the first words of the *Tao te Ching*, a basic source of the Taoist tradition and certainly one of the most priceless of the world's religious writings. These words embrace a paradox common to all religious discourse: they declare that what the book is about cannot be talked about. In the opening line of the work the author is simply informing us that he is writing a book about something no one can write about. He will use language to do something language cannot do. For eighty-one pithy chapters the *Tao te Ching* speaks of the unspeakable, but—and this is the crucial point—without ever violating that opening claim. This is language used to point beyond itself, language that wraps itself in silence.

The same insight is found throughout Buddhism, perhaps most memorably in Zen Buddhism. Whenever the Zen master is asked a direct question about the goal of the spiritual life he goes often to extreme means to express its inexpressibility: he will hit the student with a stick, or reply with manifest absurdity, or change the subject without noticing a question had been asked. And yet the enormous quantity of literature authored by Zen masters and their students is sufficient proof of the indispensability of language to their teaching. The Zen view is captured best in the well-known remark that once we have pointed to the moon the finger with which we have pointed is no longer necessary. Language is necessary—if only to make itself unnecessary. We must speak to draw someone's attention to the silence, but once we have done so the speaking may stop. We do not point to the moon in order to hold the viewer's attention to our finger.

At first glance it would appear that language in the religions of the West does not have this same paradoxical character. Judaism, Christianity, and Islam all place great emphasis on the fact that their sacred literature was *revealed*. Muslims refer to the members of all three religions as "people of the Book," and by "Book" they mean the words spoken directly by God to faithful recorders. Muslims believe that Mohammed received the Koran directly from the angel Gabriel in a series of disclosures lasting many years. For Jews the Torah was given to Moses in a personal encounter with Yahweh. For Christians the authors of the New Testament were guided by the Holy Spirit. In none of these three cases does it seem that language intends to go beyond itself, but intends rather to establish itself forever. This seems to be the finger that points at nothing but itself.

What we must note in each of these three traditions, however, is that although each has its origin in the speaking of God, the speaking of God is over. The canon is closed. Jews, Christians, and Muslims most emphatically deny the possibility that the Bible or the Koran can be revised or added to, much less substituted with a new volume of writings by modern auditors of God. There is, to be sure, much we can learn from sacred scriptures that we have not yet learned, and in that sense it may seem that something new has been revealed—but, in fact, it is only that something new has been discovered in the continuing study of a previous revelation.

The revelation as such is complete; it is only our reception of it that is incomplete. Islam puts this in the succinct claim that Mohammed is the "seal of the prophets," that is, the last person through whom God will speak. The tradition in which inspired persons may speak for God has been forever sealed.

If the speaking of God *originates* each of these traditions, we might well ask why the speaking of God does not *continue* in them, and why God does not renew and strengthen the traditions by appointing new prophets. Why is it not possible to add new laws to the Torah, or new epistles to the New Testament, or new suras to the Koran? Why has God become silent?

I am suggesting that the silence of God is not something that threatens these religions, but is an elemental reality in each of them which in fact guarantees their continuing existence. I am not implying that God has been silenced, but that God has chosen to be silent. It is not a silence into which God has disappeared, but a silence in which God is most remarkably present.

Before we can look more closely at what it means to say that God is present by way of silence, it is essential to speak to the objections certain to be raised at this point. No doubt many persons would argue that God has never ceased to speak, that the word of God as recorded in scripture is a Living Word. The grass withers and the flower fades, but the Word of the Lord endures forever. This is what scripture itself declares; why should we say that the Word of the Lord has retreated into silence? The objection is an important one, not only because many persons can be expected to raise it, but because when we look more deeply into the issue it exposes us to the necessity of God's becoming silent.

Consider two questions in response to this objection: (1) If God is still speaking through scripture how do we recognize that voice as the voice of *God*? (2) If it is the voice of God we are hearing in scripture, how do we respond to it?

(1) To begin at the most obvious and rudimentary level, we contend with the fact that the scriptures were written in a given time and place and in the vernacular of its authors. Even the most orthodox of Jews believe that it was actually Moses, David, and Solomon who wrote the bulk of the Bible. The Christian scriptures make their human authorship abundantly clear, inasmuch as most of the works bear the names of their writers, and none of them claims to have been directly or even indirectly inspired. Even if we insist that these men were mere amanuenses of God, accurately transcribing the communicated messages, it is still the case that they wrote in a natural language, with all the terminological and conceptual limitations that means. It is almost as though God is therefore limited to the vernacular idiosyncracies of a few speakers of Hebrew or Greek or Arabic. The question here is not whether God is capable of such self-limitation, but whether we can know when we are reading the words of God and when we are reading the words of Matthew and of Paul.

The simplest way out of this apparent dilemma is to say that everything contained in the Bible, *as it stands on the page*, is what God is saying. One evening, the news included a brief report on a national conference of Southern Baptists. The report opened with an excerpt from the new president's address in which he said that the task is not to adapt the Bible to the modern world but to adapt the modern world to the Bible. A young minister was interviewed on the question of the authority of the Bible. He declared in tones of complete self-assurance that the Bible is the Truth—and all we need to know of the Truth. Any attempt to alter the words of the Bible is an attempt to change God's own words and distort the truth. This is certainly one way of resolving the question as to whether God is still speaking in the scriptures, but it is a way that raises a blizzard of questions. What do we do, for example, with the discrepancies found among various texts? If we do not understand Greek, can we then not understand God? If we translate the Bible into other languages, which translations may we trust? Are some more inspired than others? How can we tell?

Perhaps the most serious question of all, concerning this simplistic approach to scripture, is whether it does not presuppose one or another catalogue of theological affirmations that have been assembled independently of any reading of the biblical text whatsoever. I am certain that these gentlemen share a wide range of beliefs on topics as diverse as homosexuality, church polity, pacifism, monogamy, political democracy, prayer in the schools, and the proper relations between the races — all of which have fragmentary or inconsistent biblical support if they have any at all. It is difficult to suppress the thought that they built their theological tower with a single language so they would not have to be confused by the many voices of scripture.

A subtler and more sophisticated way of getting at the dilemma of knowing whether we are listening to God or to Paul or to both, is to say something like "Paul wrote in Greek, but God speaks *through* the words Paul chose to set down on paper." This is analogous, say, to the way Mozart might be speaking through the notes on the page. It is not the notes that Mozart is communicating to us, but the music the notes make possible. God does not speak words, but speaks by way of words. But there is still a serious difficulty here. If God is speaking through these words, how do we know what he is saying if it is not these precise words? The problem of interpretation arises. Everyone who reads these words must interpret them, just as everyone who plays the music of Mozart is an interpreter of that music. But there is an unlimited variety of interpretations. Which shall we choose as closest to the original intention of God? It is possible to step back to another level and say that the interpretations are inspired by the same agency of God that inspired Paul. But how do we decide between conflicting interpretations, each claiming to be inspired in this secondary sense?

I do not mean these questions to be impious. On the contrary, I am only recalling an issue that rises repeatedly in scripture itself. Consider, for example, how many persons are described as having heard the words of Jesus with their own ears—without hearing the voice of God in his voice. Indeed, not even Jesus' own disciples seem to have heard it—despite the fact that they were with him day and night through a dramatic period of several years in which their lives were transformed by his presence. How else can we explain the fact that they were all dispirited at the time of his trial, then deserted him completely in his greatest suffering? What advantage do we have over these disciples? We have the words of Jesus, translated from his native Aramaic first into Greek and now into English, on the written page. The disciples heard the words of Jesus from Jesus himself, in their own native tongue. But if they could not hear what God was saying through these words, how can we be sure of interpreting them correctly?

These questions do not seem to me to be a challenge to the claim that the Bible has a divine origin. I should rather argue that the impossibility of arriving at a definitive interpretation of scripture is precisely what makes it scripture. The best we can do is to come to sacred writings from within our own human limitations, our own vernacular and conceptual biases. When we quote them we give them a meaning that is our own—not God's. To know what God means is to know God. And in the words of a fifteenth-century rabbi, Joseph Albo, "If I knew Him I would be Him." Albo was attacking the presumption that anyone has the final word on the meaning of the scripture.

(2) So far I have discussed the matter of God's silence in what we can consider epistemological terms: How can we *know* that the speaker of these words is God? How can

we know what God meant when he inspired his amanuenses to put these words to paper? There is yet another question that must be raised against the claim that God is still speaking in the scriptures: If we have been persuaded that this is the speaking of God, what do we do about it?

It is obvious enough that any persons certain they have been addressed by God will respond to that address with the deepest possible seriousness. They may feel it necessary to change their lives to conform to the message of the Living Word; or they may feel it necessary to change the lives of others. We can confidently expect that whoever receives a communication from God will regard that communication as true, and urgent, and uncompromising. In short, whoever has heard the speaking of God will thereby feel authorized to speak for God. What else *could* you do if you had heard God speak?

Recall the ironic warning of the rabbi: To know God is to be God. The implications are devastating. *To know what God is saying is to be able to speak and act as God.* It is to be the source for all true knowledge, for determining how persons should conduct their lives, who should rule and who is to be ruled.

The history of attempts to speak for God is notorious. One could reasonably argue that acting as though one had the authority of the divine is itself the very source of evil. We very seriously misunderstand the nature of evil if we think that persons act out of true malice. Virtually all evil is done in the interest of the good. If I have the word of God, straight from God, I certainly know what is good for your life, regardless of any opinions you might have concerning your life. It may even be that according to the word of the Lord as I have it that your life is to be decisively altered—or even ended altogether. I may be ordered to terminate your existence like Saul was commanded by God through Samuel to slay every last one of the Amalekites. I would not do this out of any enmity for you, of course, but out of enmity for the falsehood that has appeared in you. And what is enmity for falsehood if not a love of the truth?

There are other reasons than the recurrence of evil in history for insisting on the silence of God. If we were to gather in one place all those persons who claim to have received direct communications from God, we would be struck by the variety and the contradictory content of those various revelations. We can easily imagine the difficulty, nay, the impossibility, of getting such recipients of God's revealed word as Muhammed, Swedenborg, Joseph Smith, and Father Divine to set down a text acceptable to each.

One Friday afternoon I stayed later than usual in my office. There were no students around, and with the sun filling the room it seemed the right moment for reflection. I was presently interrupted by a loud and commanding knock at the door. "Come in," I responded, but not without some annoyance. The door opened and I looked up at a person of such startling appearance I was not certain if I were receiving a celestial visitor. Standing in the doorway was a very tall young man dressed in a flowing white garment. His considerable height was made all the more awesome by the large turban he was wearing. He asked politely but authoritatively if he could have a word with me. His manner seemed to suggest that I should rather be requesting his audience than he asking for mine. I invited him in.

He bent over somewhat to pass through the door, arranged his robe, and seated himself in a stiffly upright position directly before me. After a few moments of meditative silence he opened his eyes and began a narrative of his recent experiences in language that had a distinctly biblical cadence. I was still so unfocused by his presence, however, that I missed some of the details of his spiritual journey. What I most clearly recall is his claim not merely to have snacked at the spiritual banquet of the world's religions but to have fed his dissatisfied soul with the very meat of each great tradition. This, it happens, was not enough. He hungered for something more substantive, for the food of life itself. After a period of terrible suffering in the interior desert to which he had exiled himself, he finally opened his soul and received into it the truth of divine wisdom as it was communicated directly from the source.

He did not then proceed to disclose this truth, as I had expected, but closed his eyes again and receded behind a beatific expression—apparently contemplating it in his own silence.

"Did you write any of this down?" I asked.

He opened his eyes and replied in the way one would explain something to a child: "Oh, no. It is too precious to be carelessly abandoned to the written word. I am instructed to await the appearance of a prophet who will know how to put it into incorruptible verse."

In the piercing, searching stare that followed this remark I felt myself being examined as a possible candidate for this prophetic assignment. I tried quickly to discourage this impression by restoring a professorial tone to the exchange.

"Are you currently a student of religion?"

"I am neither student or teacher," he patiently explained, "but a master."

"A master. Mm. What is your tradition in that case? Perhaps I should ask what discipline it is of which you are a master?"

"There is only one discipline, sir. It is the discipline to the Truth. Human society is divided, but the Truth is indivisible. Human traditions are splintered by error, but there is only one Truth."

Eventually I learned the reason for this visit. The young master, whose name he never revealed to me, needed the endorsement of a professor to hold a meeting in the university's facilities. He wanted only to draw the students' attention to the errors inherent in their own religious beliefs, and to invite them into the way of Truth.

I was relieved, for this then was not a problem, at least not for me. "In that case you do not need my approval," I explained, "since there are already several groups of students who are seeking the truth through a wide variety of traditions." I named such associations as the Liberal Religious Fellowship, the Vedanta Society, and Bahai. But as I offered this list of possibilities a markedly different expression came into his face. He sat back and stared at me coldly, and shook his head ever so slightly, incredulous that I could have so completely missed his point. Though he said nothing, the logic of his previous remarks suddenly hit me. If these groups are already in existence, they must have been organized in error and ignorance; they could only be searching for something they could not understand, and would not know how to recognize even if they found it.

The man sat there for a moment in what seemed to be silent, but rather distant, rage. I had the impression it was an anger he was accustomed to, as though he expected me to disappoint him—quite like all the other ignorant, narrow, blinded persons who in their hearts despise the Truth. He sat back and looked at me as though I had shown myself to be one of them.

He said nothing more. It was a matter of simple reasoning: either I was his prophet or I was his enemy—worse, not his enemy, but an enemy of the Truth.

He raised himself from the chair, looked down at me briefly with unrelieved scorn, ducked out through the doorway, and disappeared.

In the young man's absence I found myself strangely troubled—not so much by the danger I might have been in, but by the religious implications of this bizarre event.

For one thing, I could not help wondering why it is that those who *seek* after the Truth find themselves in essential harmony, even unity, with other seekers; but those who *have* the Truth seem to have a bottomless enmity for those who do not have it, or have another truth. Why is it that our acknowledged ignorance unites us, and acknowledged possession of the Truth divides us? This young man, so clearly a partisan of the Truth, had become a sect of one, holding out against a numberless host of false believers. He was willing to face any opposition in the defense of Truth, but unwilling to join with a single other person in the search for it. (I recalled that there was something rancorous in the voice of the young Baptist minister I had heard on the radio. Possessed of the Truth, he was now looking all about him for someone he could be against.)

I wondered also whether there is a principle here that has a larger purchase. Can it be that it is what we lack, and not what we possess, that constitutes the basis for community? It seems to me that I am closer to those with whom I share an unfulfilled dream than I am to those with whom I share a realized dream. I have much more in common with persons I stand together with at the beginning of a journey than with those with whom I stand at its conclusion. Note how close the members of an athletic team are when they are in pursuit of the championship—and how easily their association dissolves after they have won it. Even if we share a rich past, what holds our communal bonds in place is the unfulfilled future for which that past is a prelude.

I was even more troubled by another reflection following my visit from the peculiar young man. In fact, I began having the kinds of thought in which we wonder whether the mind is playing tricks on itself. I actually questioned whether he had been there at all. While he was present there was not the least hint that this was an illusion, but as the light left the city outside my office window, where I still sat in reverie, I asked myself whether I had not indeed received a celestial guest.

I reviewed what I knew about the appearance of angels, particularly in biblical literature. They always come without announcement, they seem bizarre and perhaps even frightening. Angels come and go without seeming to be a part of the ongoing course of ordinary events. And usually the only persons who seem to notice their arrival are the ones to whom they have brought their message.

Later I asked the receptionist in my building whether he
happened to notice a tall, turbaned youth come in or out of my
office. No, he replied, and looked puzzled at my question.
Discreet inquiries turned up nothing. It has been ten years
and there has been no further reappearance of this figure. I
recalled how he had appeared: in spotless, almost radiant
white clothing. His enormous size also seemed significant.

But then I thought more about the biblical appearance of
angels. I remembered that the word "angel" comes from the
Greek *angelos*, which means messenger, and is closely related
to the word *euangelos*, which means good message, or gospel.
But what are the messages these figures bring? Almost without exception they are announcing that something new is
about to happen, usually a birth. They are the heralds of new
beginnings. They never bear anything that could be called the
Truth. They do not clarify the mystery of things, but awaken us
to mystery.

My young man had not spoken of beginnings; he spoke only
of conclusions. His narrative of his experiences had to do with
a successful journey, with his having come to the end of an
epic search for meaning. And the meaning he found was not
merely for himself; it was for all of us. The journey he had
completed was my journey as well as his. My search had been
terminated by his discovery.

Angels, on the other hand, invite us to adventure. They announce new departures, the beginning of an experience to
which the end is not yet in view. Abraham was in fact told by
the angel that his descendents would number as the stars in
the sky—that is, they would be beyond number, as though
what lay before him was a journey that had no end at all.

That turbaned youth was no angel. On the contrary, he was
a species of false divinity that would merely be comical if it
were not for the fact that it is to such false divinity that each
of us is somehow attracted. How often we long to have a cer-
tifiable grasp of the Truth, to be able to state the last definitive

word in debate with others. What we wish is to be able to speak as if we were God speaking, settling matters once and for all. The young man was foolish enough to wear the turban on his head where we can all see it; we are devious enough to wear the turban on our minds in the hope that it will be invisible to each other, perhaps also to ourselves. The simple fact is that if we can be turbaned giants, standing before the race, pointing out the direction history ought to take, we can continue to disregard our longing hearts.

What I am suggesting is that the silence of God does not necessarily mean that God is absent; what it *does* mean is that *we cannot present ourselves to each other as God*. Whatever other mode our speaking may take with each other, it may not take the mode of absolute truth, of divine authority. If I speak to you with the authority of God, I violate the limitations of our humanity in two ways: I regard myself as something considerably more than human, and I regard you as something considerably less than human. I see myself above error—and you helplessly caught in it. Because of God's silence I can speak to you only as the person I am, and therefore can in no way determine how you are to respond, meaning that you will answer only as the person you are.

Significantly, scripture itself returns us repeatedly to the limits of our humanity. Jesus' only direct statements about truth are directed not at his teaching, but at his person: *I am the truth*. At Jesus' trial, Pilate pauses during the proceedings to ask his prisoner a direct, perhaps even personal question: "What is truth?" Here was a remarkable opportunity. If ever there was a moment for standing before the world, and pointing out the path history should take, this was it. Here was God getting the ear of Caesar. But how did Jesus respond to this opportunity? Incredibly, he said nothing at all. Instead, he turned away in silence and went directly to his death. He followed his heart. He did not arrange the world for us; he died for us. He did not assume that he had taken our journey for us and concluded it in a way that made it forever unnecessary for us to take it on our own. He did not therefore give us a truth by which we might accordingly organize the world; he asked only that we follow him and die his death.

The point is clear and compelling. If Jesus did not arrange the world according to the truth as he knew it—and if there is any truth at all one should think that it would be fully known to the Son of God—why should we? There is a deep and tragic human tendency to think that one does not die for the truth; one kills for the truth. I do not know the man I quoted above as saying that we should adapt the world to the Bible and not the Bible to the world, but there was an anger and an arrogance in his voice that seemed ready to declare a holy war against those who place the world before the Bible. This was a man who wants the ear of Caesar, even wants to be Caesar, maybe more.

The question here is really one of intention. What is it we mean to accomplish by quoting scripture as truth, or by proclaiming truth in some other form? Is this the turbaned brute rising in us to force the world into the shape we know it should have, assigning each life its task, each nation its destiny? We may intend simply to represent God's intentions. But we do not know God's intentions. To know God is to be God.

I suggested earlier that it is the Bible's character as a provocatively varied and most human collection of writings that elevates it to the status of scripture. It begs for interpretation but defies any final, definitive interpretation. Analogous to the eternal Tao that cannot be spoken, this is the word of God that cannot be spoken as the Word of God. The Bible is the work of persons as real and as flawed as we are—fully human but only human. Therefore, when we repeat their words we do so as the real and flawed persons we are, fully human but only human. They wrote these words on the assumption that it was they and not God speaking. When we repeat them we can do so only on the assumption that it is we and not God speaking. In sum, *to quote scripture is to declare the silence of God.*

I have been suggesting that the silence of God does not necessarily mean that God is absent but that, at least from the Christian point of view, it is precisely the way God is present.

So far I have spoken of the dangers inherent in denying the silence of God, of what follows from assuming that God still speaks and one knows precisely what is said. Even if there were no dispute over the nature of this danger, however, the idea of the silence of God may still be an awkward one for the reader. For that reason it is necessary to look more closely at the nature of silence. I shall do so by distinguishing between two kinds of silence: one I shall refer to as the *silence of obedience*, and the other as the *silence of expectation*.

The silence of obedience is that which most frequently occurs in the presence of famous or powerful persons. We might applaud or cheer the entrance of the Queen or the President or the Champion, but that action is in effect a prelude to our own silence. Our applause draws attention to a special relationship between us and the honored personage. It is a way of acknowledging that when they are ready to speak we shall fall into silence—in order to listen.

I once had the good fortune, while visiting in Rome as a tourist, of being in St. Peter's one afternoon when Pope John XXIII made a scheduled entrance. I became aware of his imminent appearance only by the great number of expectant worshipers within the basilica. When guards began clearing a passageway through the crowd, there was excited speech and laughter, amounting virtually to a roar in the huge echoing spaces. When the Pope emerged minutes later, borne on his ceremonial chair, the crowd broke into deafening applause and cheers. I was shocked that this sacred space should be filled with such sounds. Nothing like this could possibly have happened in my grandmother's Methodist church. On the other hand, as the Pope passed close to where I was standing, I could see the joyful smile lighting his famous face and I broke into cheers along with all the rest. "Bravo!" I found myself yelling (of all things—as though the Pope was an opera star). "Bravo!"

Moments later he took his place at the altar, and gestured that the mass was about to begin. All noise ceased. Nowhere in that throng was there a moving body. It seemed as if everyone had even stopped breathing. When the Pope was ready to speak we became utterly silent; we became listeners only.

On another very different occasion I was standing in line one Saturday morning at a popular cheese store near my apartment. After five minutes or so I discovered that I was standing directly behind Mayor Edward Koch. I was so startled that I felt I should say something. But what should I say? I thought of "Well, if it isn't the Mayor!" But this didn't seem right. It might have been unusual for me to stand behind the Mayor, but it was not at all unique for the Mayor to stand next to any citizen of his city; he stands next to them all week. My next thought was that I could discuss cheese with him, ask him his favorite brands, and whether he likes goat cheese. But then this hardly seemed fitting since I never speak to anyone about cheese in that store, so why would I raise the subject with the Mayor? I could certainly have asked him how he was doing, or whether he was worried that something would go wrong while he was waiting for his cheese. I could have introduced myself and told him I was a voter—but then I oppose many of his policies and this did not seem like the proper place for that kind of exchange. So I stood there in silence. And I noticed that the entire store—the three clerks and the ten or twelve waiting customers—also seemed frozen in silence. (But I have noticed since that only very rarely does anyone ever talk in that store except to order cheese or to affirm their place in line.)

What is noteworthy here is not that I was silent in the

presence of the Mayor, but that I was aware of my silence. I was aware that I had nothing to say in that situation. If the Mayor had spoken I certainly would have listened, and would have quoted him word for word later. In fact, when he did order his cheese it was obvious that everyone was listening to what he ordered. To this day I recall that he bought a quantity of fontina, a variety the store offers for an unusually low price.

I have referred to this as the silence of obedience. Why *obedience*? Observe that in order to be the Holy Father or the Mayor of the City of New York one must have striven mightily. Both Mayor and Pope have had to prevail in a number of struggles. Each office does, of course, carry an enormous distinction and honor with it, but it also carries an aura of intense competition. It is achieved only by a rare skill of persuading critical constituencies of one's superiority to other candidates. Both men had made a steady climb upward through a number of other offices to reach their present high level.

Note something else. There is an almost mandatory ritual that goes with winning an important competition. No sooner is the winner declared than applause is heard in all directions. But then, as on signal, the applause ceases and the winner steps before us to give a statement about what lies ahead. Silence fills the convention hall, the cathedral. The loser, is the meantime, may also give a speech, but it can only be a declaration of loyalty to the winner, accepting the fact that the contest is over, and vowing that the loser will join with the silence of the audience. The loser concedes, in other words, the privilege of speech to the winner.

Our silence, and the silence of the loser, are ways of indicating our obedience to the winner. To be obedient is to be silent. It is to give away one's prerogative to speak for oneself in the area of the winner's new authority. In obedience we have no voice of our own. Obedience creates a silence in which our speaking has come to an end.

Of course not every aspect of our lives is covered by that obedience. It is possible to approach someone holding an office of authority as a person, ignoring the office they have won and the privilege of unchallenged speech that goes with it. I could have considered the Mayor as simply another cheese customer, and the Pope as a jolly Italian peasant. I still may not have spoken to them, but I would not have been so aware of my silence—because in that case I would not have felt required to act as audience, obedient to their authority. Obedience, in other words, and the silence that goes with it, is a response to the office and not to the person who holds it.

The silence of obedience we may feel before God is not different in kind, only in scope. If we consider God in the office of King, of Mighty Fortress, of Ruler of All Things Seen and Unseen, of our Shield and Avenger, we not only give up any claim to our own speech, we also believe that every aspect of our lives is covered by God's authority. We stand before him as utter losers whose silence is a form of humiliation. What is most important here is that when we are overwhelmed with the offices of God—and notice how often they are competitive in spirit, even warlike—we have no way of addressing the person of God. There is nothing remotely like God's being a cheese customer or an Italian peasant.

The *silence of obedience*, in other words, is that form of silence which brings our speech to an end. The *silence of expectation*, on the other hand, is just the opposite: it is the silence that makes speech possible. The intuitive idea behind the latter form of silence is a simple one: unless we have someone to speak to we cannot speak, and unless someone is listening there is no one to whom we can speak.

This is a familiar theme in the contemporary philosophy of language. We cannot actually speak to ourselves. I cannot speak to myself any more than I can steal from myself, or make myself richer by placing the dollar I have in one hand into the other. If I had no one to talk to I would quite literally have to give up talking—except perhaps to continue in the sort of meaningless babble we call "talking to ourselves," a characteristic of insanity—and what is much worse, I would eventually cease having anything to say.

Therefore, unless someone offers me a silence in the form of their listening I cannot speak. I am quite dependent on their silence to be able to say anything at all. I refer to this as the silence of expectation because it is a silence in which I am expected to speak. Another person has stopped speaking, has turned toward me with an invitation to speak, and is waiting for my words.

This is a matter of great human importance. Imagine what would happen if all the persons about you ceased to listen. Your own speech could be addressed to no one. You would have nothing to say. You may resort to violence or conspicuous and bizarre behavior with the intention of making others take notice of you and listen. If they continue to be deaf to you even those actions become meaningless. You become so isolated that even your own thinking will be useless. It is by no means difficult to see how one can effectively vanish into such a silence, ceasing actually to exist at all. To offer something of a variation on Descartes's famous formula, it is not because I think, but because I am heard, that I am.

Circumstances in which a person is sealed off into such a silence is not so rare as one might think. Indeed, it may even be a most common condition. It occurs wherever a person must relate only to those who consider themselves winners of some kind, who speak as holders of an office to an audience of losers. How common it is in families for parents not to speak *to* their children, but to speak *for* them without the merest regard for what the children might want to say for themselves. The same phenomenon occurs in the relations between employer and workers, between teacher and students, between one race or culture and another.

The implication here is that the person who does listen, who does turn toward me in the silence of expectation, has given up any claim to superiority and has in fact emptied himself or herself of any sort of office I must stand before in silent obedience. A genuine silence of expectation can occur only when one person listens to another in a circumstance of equal and shared humanity.

It is a central claim of Christians that God has become incarnate in the person of Jesus, empty of all official claims to divinity, sharing with us every aspect of our humanity even unto humiliation and death. God has come before us as a listener, and waits in silence for us to speak. This is another way of saying that Jesus refused to live beyond the limits of his humanity. By passing up the chance to speak as God to Caesar the silence in which Jesus went to his death becomes a powerful silence of expectation. He did not speak for us, but left everything still to be said by us.

The Gospel of John, the only gospel in which Pilate's question as to truth is reported, opens with the famous words: In the beginning was the Word, and the Word was with God, and the Word was God. What is important for us to understand here is that the great Christian proclamation is not that the Word of God became written down and left itself in the form of scriptural truth, but that the Word of God became flesh and dwelt among us full of grace and truth.

The preceding account of the distinction between the silence of obedience and the silence of expectation has implied a similar distinction between two kinds of speaking. In the one instance, I speak to make you silent, in the other, I speak to give you voice. When I speak to your silent obedience I demand that you listen to me in such a way that you have no voice except what I authorize you to have. When I speak expectantly, as one who shares in all the limitations of your mortal existence, I invite you to respond in a voice that can only be yours.

Speech in the imperative mode is therefore contradictory. It is speech meant to end speech. The imperative speaker has no one to speak to, only persons to speak for—or persons whose voice is but an extension of the master's. If imperative speech is successful there results a silence so complete that there is nothing more to be said. *Sicut dixit dominus.* Thus speaks the lord.

Speech in the expectant mode is not contradictory but reciprocal. In speaking to you expectantly I do not intend to bring your speaking to an end, but to bring my own speaking to an end—and to bring it to an end in such a way that it makes your speaking possible. The reciprocity consists in the fact that if you do not respond to what I have said, I have not spoken to you at all. If you remain silent I have not offered you my silence—either because I have not drawn your attention to my silence, or because I have continued speaking and am therefore not silent at all. I so completely depend on your response that if my speaking does not transform itself into a listening I have not spoken. I have simply uttered words, mere sounds, into uncomprehending space.

This may seem to put speakers of expectation at a great disadvantage, for the only way they can communicate with others is through silence. Their speaking has no power in itself. Their words cannot move listeners to a desired end. They cannot have the slightest influence over listeners, for if they do they have moved from an expectational to an imperative mode. If you speak what I want you to speak it can only be because I have given you my voice and compelled yours to be silent.

On the other hand, though the speech of expectation is not powerful in the ordinary way, it is creative in an extraordinary way. In order to listen to me it is not enough for you to sit before me waiting quietly. You must indicate somehow what you are listening for. Your expectation must point me toward certain possibilities of speech. Such pointing occurs subtly, and involves a disclosure on your part as to what it is in me to which you will be receptive. You may reveal your receptivity verbally, or through other gestures that indicate an area of openness between us.

It is always the case that when someone listens to you with genuine openness you will find a voice to say what you have never been able to say before, and did not know you could have said. This is not simply having new words to say; it is rather an expanding, an opening toward oneself, an awakening of the heart. This could be put in even stronger terms. It is not that sensitive listening will lead you to *discover* a new depth to yourself; it will *create* a new depth. This is why listening, why speaking expectantly, is creative. I am heard therefore I am. I am who I am only because I have been heard.

What then shall we say of God? If we are to insist that God is an imperative speaker, then what God is reported to have said is still authoritative and we should give away our own voice to repeat it. On the face of it we might easily assume that if God were really speaking *as God*, it would only be in the role of a supremely imperative speaker. We can well imagine that if God truly spoke to us the entire earth would go silent, more silent still than the cheese store with the mayor in it. But this would put God in the strangest dilemma. By filling our minds and mouths with God's own words we are left with nothing to say. God could only speak for us, having changed us into an extension of the divine voice. This is quite the same as saying that if God speaks as God there will be no one there to listen, that God will be speaking only to God, and therefore will not be speaking at all. God is under the same impossibility that we are in being unable to speak to ourselves.

If we should say that God has not spoken imperatively, but expectantly, then we read the revealed word, or scriptures, very differently. We should see in them an indication of what God listens for in us. Is there a revealed receptiveness here that can create in us a new heart?

It must be said at once that scriptures never come to us on the printed page alone, as though we could grasp them completely in isolation. Scriptures belong to a community of persons who respond to the written word and to each other with their own expressions of receptivity. Scriptures cannot be read without being interpreted—even if one intends to read them as though God were still speaking these words—and the interpretation is always the way by which readers disclose their receptivity to others. It is their way of listening, or refusing to listen. Great interpreters are not persons who have found the true meaning of the text and set it out so clearly and persuasively that all further interpretation is unnecessary. Great interpreters are those who inspire others to voice their own response to the text; who enable others to say what they had never known it possible to say.

Of course, the same point can be made of Shakespeare, Nagarjuna, Tolstoy, Homer, or Dickens. They, too, have spoken and then dropped back into the silence, making way for our response. Indeed, it is the depth and frequency of response to these writers that constitute their greatness. Is there something about the Bible that makes it more authoritative than other writings? It is plainly not possible that there could be independent evidence giving priority to the Bible, for such evidence would have the status of divine authority and put us back into the position of speaking imperatively. What distinguishes the Christian scriptures—and here they have much in common with other great scriptural texts—is not that they contain a greater truth, but that they seem to search us more deeply. They lead us into a more comprehensive silence, as though there is no part of our existence that is not called upon to speak in response. The biblical writers prepare the way for us to speak of beauty, of social justice, of faith, of moral conduct, of the terror of death and the pain of grief, of a hope for renewed life, of a meaning to history. What is remarkable about the Bible is not that it presents a systematic and compendious statement of the truth that provides in advance for every possible argument against it, but that, on the contrary, it speaks with so many voices. These voices have gone silent, but it is a deeply provocative and engendering silence that calls us to voices of our own. It is a creative kind of speaking that becomes silent in a way that opens to us a possibility of saying what we could not have said before being confronted. By creating in us a new voice it creates a new heart. We become new beings. It is no surprise that the theologians have come to speak of scripture as the work of the Holy Spirit. The word *spiritus* means breath; we cannot be enspirited except by way of our own voice.

Imagine what would happen if the Bible presented a perfectly clear, unified conception of human and divine affairs, requiring essentially no further interpretation because its meanings were all quite lucid and accessible in a variety of languages. It is not difficult to see that they would have vanished after their first publication. Like the instructions that come with unassembled toys, they would have become useless and superfluous once they had been understood. What distinguishes scripture is not that it is unclear or useless, but that it repeatedly brings its interpreters to the possibility of speaking from their own hearts.

To insist on the present silence of God is merely to say that whatever authority we claim for the Bible, however we might argue that the origin of these words is divine, God is no longer speaking them. If they are spoken at all, we speak them. If we speak them, it is because we are responding to the silence of God. How we respond to the silence of God has entirely to do with how we are being listened to. My own suggestion is that the apparently endless variety of interpretative responses to scripture shows how thoroughly we can be listened to. It awakens us to the most intimate voice of the heart. It is because our hearts find their voice that the present silence of God has become the silent presence of God.

But the heart, as I stressed earlier, is a beggar. Its essential mode is one of petition. It cannot live except by asking for life. This is to say that when the silence of God opens us to the voice of the heart, the only possible response is prayer.

Before looking more directly at prayer itself, and giving more substance to the claim that the heart is a beggar, I want to conclude this meditation by commenting briefly on the suggestion that interpretation prepares us for prayer. It is unlikely that many interpreters would understand what they are doing in such terms. Most interpretation seems self-consciously to be *about* something, in this case the Bible. It is the kind of activity I referred to earlier as theology. As such it is concerned with clarifying obscurities in the text, discovering its historical setting, making obvious the views of its authors, and correcting the errors commonly made by other readers of the text. Insofar as it is a theological and historical task it is concerned with providing true information, accurate readings of pivotal verses, generally eliminating the misleading and distorted interpretations of others. In other words, there is a tendency in all interpretation of this kind toward imperative speech, toward achieving the silence of obedience in its readers and listeners.

Interpretation can certainly be done in the mode of expectation. When it is, its effect is not to silence its readers and listeners but to encourage them to become interpreters themselves. This means, of course, that all struggle for right or true interpretation is set aside, all attempts to get the accurate meaning of the text are dropped. The most effective interpretation is that which invites the broadest variety of interpretations in response.

Am I saying then that *any* interpretation will do, that we are faced with an insuperable relativism in which the most desultory reader can offer an interpretation that has no less authority than that of the most concentrated scholar? Not at all. Interpretation in the mode of expectation comes from the heart. It is not an attempt to restate what scripture says, but a way of calling each other to the *spiritus* of its silence. The variety of interpretations does not therefore voice its power but reveals its great creativity. Each new interpretation of scripture that is intended to reduce some of its mystery only has the effect of showing its mystery to be more inexhaustible than we had thought.

I want to say again, more emphatically than before, that God's mysteriousness, or the resistence of God to our attempts to speak for God, is not a hindrance to prayer; it is its indispensable ground. Authoritative knowledge about something may seem to be an advantage, but in fact it has the effect of masking one's heart. It makes it possible for us to speak to God *about* something, and in doing so we ask for nothing. Authoritative knowledge also shapes in advance what one is to ask for, but when requests are shaped by something other than the true longing of the heart they are no longer one's own requests.

There are no formulae for prayer. In genuine prayer I say only what I want to say, and say only what I want.

What We Can Properly Ask of God

There is a difficulty in my first meditation on the silence of God I know I have not faced. Even if it is agreed all around that we cannot speak for God, even if we all see clearly that to know God is to be God, it still happens that I am speaking a good deal about God in these meditations. How do I know enough about God even to say that God is silent? Is it enough to argue that just because we hear nothing from God there is a God who is saying nothing? This seems analogous to concluding that because we hear nothing on the other side of the closed door there is not someone waiting for us to knock.

Theologians have a customary way of resolving this difficulty. They say that faith precedes knowledge. It is one thing to *know* God is there in the silence, it is another to *have faith* that God is there. Virtually all the church's greatest thinkers have adopted a principle that first appears in the writing of St. Augustine (354–430): *Understanding follows faith*. We do not believe what we are already able to understand, but attempt to understand that in which we have faith.

The fact that knowledge, or understanding, does not come before faith means inevitably that faith entails risk. The risk entailed in faith is of a very special sort; it involves no calculation. Faith is not the activity of determining the degree of likelihood that God is there—as though one might decide the chances are better than fifty-fifty and then believing if it seems prudent. The emphasis in faith is on the willingness to risk, not on the chances of losing your wager.

Most matters in the realm of the spirit are paradoxical. In worldly affairs, where we calculate our risks, relying on paradox would bring us to certain ruin. We might invest money in a long-shot business venture if it also offers the possibility of very high payoff. We might be ruined by doing so, but there is a certain amount of reason for taking such action. It seems like a smart gamble. There is no gambling in the spirit. One does not risk oneself spiritually in the hope of a profitable outcome. *The risk is itself the outcome.* This is the paradox. If you want to save your life, you must first lose it. The issue in faith is not, then, whether there is anyone beyond the door, but whether we can drop everything to knock on it. The door will most certainly open—but only to that person who risks everything without the least concern for gain.

The most perfect biblical image of faith is that of Abraham proceeding directly to the sacrifice of his son, though he was about to destroy something far more valuable to him than his own life. No wonder Abraham is known ever after as the father of faith.

The relation of prayer to faith is vividly captured in a short scene in the Gospel of Mark. A father has brought his epileptic son to Jesus, begging Jesus to "have pity on and help us." Jesus replied by a declaration of the paradox: "All things are possible to him who believes." The father's remarkable response was to cry out, "I believe; help my unbelief!" The crucial term here is not *belief*, but *help*. What confirms the authenticity of the father's faith is not that he first believed and then asked, but that he asked directly from his heart. The reference to his unbelief seems to suggest that he may not even have believed that Jesus was able to do what he asked. If he had calculated the chances of getting the boy cured of his terrible affliction he may have found that they were not all that good. In fact, the father had already pled with Jesus' disciples to heal his son, and they had tried but failed. Now, coming to Jesus himself, the father disregards the odds and asks for everything as though his very life depended on it. Later, the disciples asked Jesus why they had not been able to heal the boy. He said simply that this kind of illness "cannot be driven out by anything but prayer."

There are countless examples in Christian history of persons whose lives are dramatized by their willingness to risk everything. Certainly among the most colorful are the early Irish monks who would go so far as to put out to sea in small craft, merely to drift wherever the tides and the winds would take them. They considered themselves *peregrini*, pilgrims or wanderers. They were giving outward form to the spiritual act of placing themselves at God's mercy. Far from any landfall, without chart or rudder, they were left with nothing but the cry of the epileptic's father: Help! Of course, if their intention had been to isolate themselves physically in a way that would give the cry of help authenticity, they would have been frauds. Their wandering was spiritually genuine only if it reflected a recognition that in their human condition they were already at sea and without any resource to save themselves.

All of this illustrates the theological point that faith is greater than knowledge, and that we do not need to know if anyone is beyond the door before we set down all that we carry, all our burdens and treasures, and knock on it. To be sure, by insisting on this, theologians make theology a tentative enterprise. It is a kind of knowledge that knows it cannot count. I am repeating the observation made in the Introduction that theology is joyful discourse among persons who have rushed to the door, or put to sea in their diminutive vessels. Theology succeeds when it fails; that is, when the theologian's journey is not so successful that it eliminates the need for your own, but so suggestive that it invites you to set forth on your own. In the same way, the speaking of God in these meditations is a tentative speaking, a nonknowing knowing; an attempt to listen, to speak, and to listen again.

The matter that now asks for comment is the rush to the door, the initial cry of the heart into the enormous silence — a cry that precedes all other wants and passions. The question is what can we ask of God that we can ask *only* of God.

In the Introduction to this book I indicated that the word *praying* has virtually the same meaning as *begging*, probably its closest synonym. To understand prayer as begging it may be helpful to contrast it with *desiring*, sometimes confused with praying since they are both a form of asking for something. It is one thing to beg, quite another to desire. The father of the epileptic did not desire to have his son healed, he begged for healing.

The most elemental difference between begging and desiring is that in begging we ask for what we cannot live without, but have no resources of our own to obtain. We do not beg unless our lives are in jeopardy. At bottom then all begging is a begging for life. Desire, on the other hand, is focused on an object one can quite well live without, even if it causes acute dissatisfaction. I do not desire to exist, but to exist in some other time and place, perhaps even as another person. Therefore, what I desire I cannot beg for because my existence is not at stake.

If prayer is to be understood as begging, and not mere desiring, it may seem that we are only rarely in a circumstance where prayer is appropriate. It does seem that there are very few moments in a *well-organized life* when we are brought to the extreme of having to beg for our existence. I have emphasized the phrase "well-organized life" to draw attention to the deep habit of looking ahead in life, heading off the disasters that reduce us to begging. For myself I have the example of the Irish monks — those holy wanderers, charming and a bit exotic—but they are an example I hesitate to follow. Frankly, I am a habitual chart man. I trust as little as possible to the tides and winds.

But in doing so I deceive myself. Being preoccupied with charts is a way of forgetting that I am a frail craft indeed, and by no means a master over the histories through which I am trying to navigate. If we look behind this common deception we find that begging is not an occasional necessity, and a misfortune; it is of the very essence of what it means to be human. The truth is, *we can have nothing we do not ask for.*

Now I know this observation seems overstated, and in fact seems false on the face of it. If I have something I obviously no longer have to ask for it, and if I am asking for something it is clear enough that I do not yet have it. And in one very important matter, I must say that the life I have I did not ask for— who, after all, asks to be born? But I mean the statement to be taken literally in both cases: I can have material possessions only by continuing to beg for them, and I cannot be born without asking to be born.

Consider first the question of material possessions. It is true in a formal sense that I cannot ask for what I already have, but, on the other hand, I must ask to *keep* what I already have; that is, to continue having it. I can continue to have only what others *permit* me to have. In this sense my possessions are mine only to the degree that others agree to my ownership. It is true that I can lock our apartment in the city and go away for weeks at a time, certain that nothing will be missing when we return, and that this fact encourages us to believe that our possessions are indisputably ours, and depend on no one's agreement. However, the powerful lock on the front door was installed by an expert on whose skill we must depend. There is a security system in our building, and a doorman whose responsibility is to see that no one enters our apartment and steals anything. In our daily coming and going in the city we depend on many others. We cannot walk the streets, or drive an automobile, or make a purchase, or express political opinions, except where others suffer us to do so.

Even money itself, often thought to be an irresistable form of power, is only paper or metal, and *becomes* money only when persons agree to use it as such. When we offer money to others for their property or labor we receive in return not what the money forces them to do, but what they *offer* in exchange. That is, we must beg them to accept our money in exchange for something of theirs.

The point here is that there can be no such thing as material possessions without a subtle and complicated network of societal agreements. We must all consent to an enormous number of social practices before any of us can have anything at all. What is most important here is that unless there is a collective will to sustain these agreements we are individually helpless. I cannot independently decide to have the kind of society I want, but must live in that which has already been shaped by a collective will. This is not to say that, except in rare instances, I can have no influence over my social environment. But those influences inevitably take the form of a plea that my own needs be respected. I must beg to be listened to. To be able to have anything that I can call my own, therefore, I must live in my society as a suppliant. All social bond involves a form of prayer.

If it is true that we can have nothing we do not ask for, it is also true that *no one can give us what we do not ask for.* No matter how much I might desire to give you money or some other property, if you do not accept it from me I am powerless to make you do so. I make this point to emphasize the thorough reciprocity of our social relations. In this connection we can also see quite clearly how this interdependence includes nonmaterial as well as material exchanges. I cannot be human at all unless I am listened to, unless others respond to me out of their own spontaneity. I cannot demand that someone love me, or despise me. What is more, if I do not want your love, or your admiration, or even your anger, there is simply no way you could give them to me. You might, of course, feel them, perhaps acutely, but insofar as they remain only feelings they are not genuine personal exchanges. You have given me nothing. How deeply frustrating, and dissatisfying, it is to express your affection, or your rage, at someone who does not respond to it in any discernible way. At such moments we can see how much we depend on others asking for our expressions.

We cannot have what we do not beg for, and we cannot be given what we do not beg for. So far I have discussed this principle in terms of material and nonmaterial possessions. But earlier I stressed that begging is at bottom a begging for life itself. Can we say that we cannot have life, or even be given life, without begging for it? This is the point at which we must contend with the truism that we did not ask to be born.

In one sense, but in a very limited sense, it is true that we do not initiate the physiological process that results in our material existence. But then it is also true that while we cannot be the persons we are without our bodies, we are not the persons we are *as* those physical entities. The term, reproduction, is quite misleading here, since it implies that parents *produce* children, duplicating precisely the means by which they were produced. This suggests that as persons we are the outcome, or the result, of an autonomous process extending back indefinitely into the past. According to this way of thinking we are who we are quite independently of the persons around us. A literary critic once said of the characters of Dickens that they were so completely conceived by him before he located them in his stories that they were incapable of inner growth of development. They did not speak with each other, he said, so much as collide with each other without ever altering the pattern of words and actions their author assigned them. The critic did not have to add that Dickens should have known better. None of us springs as finished persons from the author's imagination. The language we speak is not scripted in advance, but must be learned from those who were speaking it before we were conceived. Recall the earlier point that it is simply nonsensical to say that we have language all by ourselves, for that would mean it would be possible to speak with ourselves, which we could no more do than steal from the left hand what we hold in the right. So, too, with all our social involvements. We were not born brave, or funny, or melancholy. Each of these terms describes the way we interact with others, and makes no sense when applied to one in isolation. I cannot be brave all by myself.

In other words, everything that constitutes us as persons can be found only in active and reciprocal social relations. Unless others reach out to me, unless others listen, I cannot be a person. At the same time, I must also reach out to others, I must be a listener myself. I cannot be a person unless the possibility is offered me by others. But those others are powerless to *make* me a person. I must ask for what they offer; I must beg them to listen.

It is true of even the smallest infant that our love for it is utterly without effect unless it asks to have that love of us. That is why parenting is so enormously difficult. We are often prepared to give a great many things to a child—before the child has asked for them. And what the child truly asks for we may not hear, or be able to give in response.

The great difference between parents and children is not that the parents have so much more to give, but that the children have so much more to ask for. Childhood is a time of great dependence; that is to say, *need*, and therefore a time of begging from others. There is no more complete hunger than that of the newborn. They are asking not only for a material sustenance which they cannot obtain on their own, but they are asking for a great many forms of human touching of the very most fundamental and unconditional sort. Childhood is a state of the purest hunger for life. It is a state of being that can be comprehended as uninterrupted prayer.

As children mature toward adulthood the greatest changes they undergo are not the possession of more and more, but the inclination to ask for less and less. The very definition of adulthood is one of self-sufficiency; it is a time of life in which we are expected to provide our own sustenance, come to our own political and moral decisions, choose the future course of our lives—all with the least possible amount of instruction or support from others. It is in adulthood that the hunger for life gives way to the appetite for a different life. It is simply not adult to ask for help except in ways that do not damage our basic self-sufficiency. In other words, the older we get the more we are expected to become like Dickens's characters: fixed, closed to change, more likely to collide with others than grow with them.

The other way to say this is that the greatest difference between adults and children is not that adults have more but that they can receive less. Since as adults we ask for little we can receive little.

The conclusion to this way of thinking is that we do indeed ask to be born *as the persons we are*. But now we have a deeper sense of what birth means. It is not something that occurs to us from without, but something that has to do with the way we are from within. I cannot claim to have been born until I ask others for the possibility of life. This, in turn, means that the cry for help does not depend on my birth, but my birth on the cry for help. Therefore, my birth renews itself whenever I reach out anew for life. To act openly on the knowledge of absolute dependence on others is to experience rebirth, the renewing of life. Birth is not therefore to be thought of as the outcome of a physiological process, but the beginning of an uncharted journey.

The question before us in this meditation is what we can properly ask of God. I have been exploring the fact that praying and begging are essentially synonymous, attempting to show that begging is not an unfortunate necessity that arises in the ill-planned life, but the very possibility of life itself. I began by making a distinction between begging and desiring. I also indicated provisionally that begging and desiring differ in much the same way that hunger and appetite differ. We need now to look more deeply into the nature of desiring because it is desire that creates the most resistant obstacle to genuine prayer.

Desire arises from within—no one *forces* desire on another—but is always focused on an object without. It begins with a perception of what we lack and then fastens its attention on what is required to make up the lack. It may well be, of course, that there is considerable vagueness about the object being sought out of desire, but it is always the case that the existence of desire rests upon the assumption that there is an object somewhere that will satisfy it. Sexual desire, for example, can be entirely focused on another person, or it can be so abstract as to seek out a single action that essentially anyone could provide. But it is always in search of something outside itself.

Very soon we come to see in the structure of desire a simple and obvious contradiction: *it is the goal of desire to end itself.* By seeking an object that can satisfy our desire we are simply attempting to eliminate that desire itself.

This self-eliminating chracteristic of desire has an especially poignant consequence. *Once we have succeeded in acquiring the object of desire, that object is no longer desirable.* We want to have something which we will no longer want. The simplest example here might be money. I am acutely aware that I am working for money. I know precisely how much I earn, and I am frequently keen on increasing that amount by appealing to my Dean or looking about for extra employment. Whatever attitudes I have toward this bald form of greed, I cannot deny that money is something I want. On the other hand it is quite obvious, upon reflection, that it is *not* the money I want. For if it were only money I am working for I would be happy to bring home my salary in coins, and store them indefinitely. The contradiction rises at once here, for no sooner do I have the money I want than I want something else by way of the money. In fact, I want to get rid of the money as quickly and as efficiently as possible and replace it with other wanted objects.

The simple fact is that the satisfaction of desire is dissatisfying. This produces something of a dilemma. I must somehow decide what is to be done with the acquired objects of my desire that I no longer desire. What I have observed is that there seem to be two major strategies for dealing with these now unwanted objects. One is to make them a basis for new desires; another is to make them desirable to others.

According to the first strategy, I waste as little time as possible using the money I have accumulated to get possession of something else I desire. We must be careful to describe this strategy as it is usually employed. I give a false impression if I describe money as something I discover I do not want once I have it. I know well in advance that it is not the money itself I desire. The money is something I will unload as quickly as possible for the sake of, say, having a safe and attractive apartment in New York City. The dilemma, naturally, repeats itself at once. The apartment is not an end in itself; it is not really the apartment I want. I want to have a place where we can be proud to entertain friends, and where each of us can pursue our personal and vocational interests without distraction from the others. But the worm of this contradiction is tireless, for it makes its way into these goals as well. It compels me to ask what I want from my friends, and from my professional successes.

So long as we preoccupy ourselves with the satisfaction of desire our lives are haunted with disappointment, for we seem never to be able to get what we really want. As a result we look around for new objects of desire, hoping that there is something of such value that it remains forever desirable and we forever wanting it. What we do, in effect, is to do whatever is possible to keep ourselves in a state of desire. This strategy is deeply enshrined in our civilization—and by no means an invention of the modern consumer society. Its most colorful appearance in antiquity is probably the Roman invention of the vomitorium, a facility placed in the finest homes, where guests could empty themselves of their recently consumed meal in the interest of returning to the table with a freshened appetite. These Romans were not interested in satiating themselves but in remaining gluttonous as long as possible. They practiced a subtle art of fueling their desires by offering them objects easily gotten rid of.

The vomitorium has disappeared from homes and restaurants, to be sure, but it has not disappeared from the human spirit. Indeed, modern consumer society can be understood as an institutionalized vomitorium. Like the Romans we want something that will not sate our appetites in discomfort and torpor, but will sharpen them, leading us as eagerly to the next course as to the previous. We are all familiar with the appetite for money, but it is obvious that this is an appetite that is not satisfied by money. On the contrary, the only reason for this appetite is that money can lead us to new wants, it can be vomited away without damaging our appetites. We do not desire money then, but what money can acquire for us: a lovely home, say, or a handsome automobile, an excellent education. But none of these is sought as the terminus of a quest; each is the basis for still new desires. Why should I have a beautiful home if not for the anticipated pleasures that it might provide?

The contradictoriness of desire is such a universal phenomenon that examples can be found all about us. Clever advertisements never sell the objects of desire, they sell the desire their objects make possible. Consider the extensive pornography industry for one, which has almost nothing to do with the satisfaction of desire. On the contrary, it thrives on the illusion that desire can be endlessly increased, and exercises its greatest skills in eliciting desires we never before experienced. In this sense pornography is not a blight on the culture, a kind of social rot weakening the moral foundations of the civilization; it is the most successful exercise of the very principle on which essentially all respectable commerce is built: not fulfilling desire, but exciting it.

I cannot reflect on this point without recalling a painfully revealing experience of satisfied desire during my youth. I was nineteen years old and had just returned from my second year of college. As a sort of ceremonial recognition of the passage of this moment my parents took my younger brother and sister and me out to dinner at a restaurant somewhat more fashionable than we were used to. After we had dined we came out into the warm summer night to discover that a full moon had arisen, throwing a spectral beauty over the restaurant lawn and parking lot. Strolling casually out to the car with our after-dinner cigars, my brother and I were simultaneously captured by what seemed at first to be a vision. There, parked all by itself in the radiant moonlight, was a red Ford convertible with white sidewalls, white leather seats, and a chrome spare tire case. The year was 1951. I have no doubt that the Ford designers surpassed themselves with this creation, and I still believe they have never again achieved anything so nearly sublime. It was low and raked back, the very image of power and grace. My sister and my parents also must have admired this rare work of automotive beauty, but all I remember is that my brother and I were swept into a frenzy of covetousness and envy. With a kind of rage I realized that someone actually owned this car, and would eventually come out to drive it away into a June night of endless excitement. We walked around it several times, aching with the thought that one day, years away, we might actually live in such an eternal June.

The ache lasted for days. The fact that I had to spend my summer working the night shift in an iron foundry to pay for my next year at college certainly helped to keep the pain alive. About two weeks later my brother and I, on our way home after a golf game in our own decrepit old car, turned the corner at our house and found this very Ford convertible parked in the driveway. Its low red body, the white leather seats, and the chrome spare wheel tire case gleamed like flame in the evening sun. Could it be, we asked each other as we raced into the house, that the owner of this dream is actually visiting our father? But nobody was there; only my sister and parents sitting quietly in the living room.

"Oh." My brother sighed with disappointment. "We thought the guy that owns that car was here."

"He is," my father replied. He lifted the keys off a side table and tossed them in our direction. "The car is yours. Now you had better try it out before dinner, because if you don't like it there is still time to return it to the dealer before he closes for the night."

The summer was transformed. When we were not working we were in that car gliding about town, casting the shadow of envy in every direction. I quickly became familiar with the way persons in other cars looked at us as we sped past them; they looked at us at an angle as though they did not want us to notice we were being looked at. Every friend we ever had suddenly became our best friend. Girls never seemed to have any other dates or commitments. Suddenly, working in the foundry was no longer odious. We waxed and polished every square inch of the car, even keeping the engine free of grease and dust.

Near the end of the summer I was driving my father around on a couple of errands. As we stopped at a light he turned to me and asked, "Do you want to know why I gave you boys this car?"

His question was astonishing and disturbing. I thought I knew why he had given us the car. My father was by no means a rich man; I knew the car had meant a tremendous sacrifice. I also knew that impulsive, grand gestures of this sort were characteristic of him. I thought he had given us the car on a gallant whim, for no other reason than the desire of his sons to possess it. So why the question?

"Yes," I answered, tentatively. "Why?"

He hesitated a moment, then spoke slowly with quiet emphasis. "So you would never want it again."

A week later we were off to college, but since we went to different schools, my brother and I had to work out an elaborate plan for sharing the car. This was done amicably enough, but I noticed each time I got the car it required more attention than I had expected. My brother might have failed to change the oil. It seemed to have been driven too hard. When I complained to him he pointed out that I usually left the inside of the car a mess. It seemed easier to let my brother have the car for the entire spring term. When he came home with it for the summer vacation it was scratched here and there and badly needed waxing. At the end of the summer my father sold it. Nobody protested. In fact, I can recall no reaction at all when I learned it had been sold.

When I think back to this experience I am amazed at how successfully my father's plan worked, if indeed it was as conscious a plan as his question under the traffic light suggested. The truth is that I have no unanswered yearning for that car. I have not seen one like it in many years, and suspect that if I were to come across one somewhere I would have some sense of loss. But it is not the loss of the car that I would experience. What I miss more than that car, and more even than that long summer of perfect evenings, is the exquisite covetousness I felt in the restaurant parking lot. I want to stand in the moonlight again and believe that there is something that could satisfy every desire yet remain desirable. I do not want that car any more than the Romans wanted their meat and wine. I want the wanting of it.

I have been considering one of the ways in which we resolve the dilemma we find ourselves in when the objects of desire, once possessed, have lost their appeal. This is the belief that one day we will discover the very object that will satiate all our desire while simultaneously fueling it. Under the influence of this belief we become acutely dissatisfied with what we have and restlessly look about for something still more desirable — whether it be a new car, a new lover, a trimmer and healthier body, or a different job. This belief even affects the way we think about God, inclining us toward metaphors in which God becomes a home for the wandering soul, or a source of eternal and inexhaustible delight. By this way of thinking God is the most desirable of all objects, and our restless hearts will have no rest until they rest in God. It is as though having been repeatedly disappointed by life we will not be disappointed by God. But there is a terrible despair in this view, for it is a vigorous rejection of what we have already been given; it is an implicit admission that God has already deeply disappointed us. As we shall see more fully, the life of prayer has a very different intention, for it is an opening to what we are currently being given and therefore has no place in itself for disappointment.

There is at least one other strategy for dealing with the contradictoriness of desire. If we cannot continue to desire what we have come to possess we can attempt to display what we have so as to make it desirable to others. Of course, it will be desirable to them only so long as they cannot have it; only so long, that is, as we withhold it from them. I have no doubt at all that if everyone who wanted one could have a red Ford convertible, I should not have wanted mine at all. Even if anyone who wished to do so could have driven our convertible around town I am certain I would have lost interest. My brother and I owned something that many others coveted, but could not have — and for that reason we wanted it. The continuing desirability of that car depended on the fact that the two of us had it *against* others. Our ownership was an opposition, an effective denial of the wishes of others.

But the opposition that all ownership implies rarely wears

such an antagonistic face. My brother and I skillfully hid any odor of hostility by acquiring the style of easy generosity. We regularly invited others to join in on our good fortune. We wanted them to enjoy this boon with us. All the same, the car remained ours, all decisions concerning it were ours alone. No one else had the privilege of generosity. But there was nothing malevolent in our motivation. We wished no one harm. On the contrary, we had the sunniest possible dispositions, quite convinced that we were a treasured source of delight for the suddenly large number of friends.

This view of our own actions, however, errs decisively. The contradictoriness of desire was holding us in a double grip. If we could no longer desire to have what we now owned unless others coveted it, we nonetheless had to appear as though we had what we wanted, else others would not be covetous. Therefore our high spirits and manifest pleasure in this new style of life rested largely on our ability to convince others to believe what we knew to be false. I cannot, of course, speak for my brother in this matter, but I do most clearly remember my own intentions—and they were hardly exceptional for a nineteen year old. I wanted to appear everywhere in that dazzling car as a shirtless, blond, muscular, carefree youth who had life exactly where he wanted it, and not as the kind of unlucky fellow who had to work nights in an iron foundry to pay for his college tuition.

The simple word for this management of desire is *seduction*. Seduction always implies deception. In the process of seducing others we want them to acquire a desire for an object over which we have control—and have no intention of giving up. It is irrelevant whether the object in question is one's money, or property, or social status. Even if it is one's body that is offered as the object of desire, it is a mistake to think that the seducer actually *gives* his or her body to another. As much as our automobile was used by others in any number of ways we never gave it to anyone. In my own case, what I was pretending to offer my friends was not just the car, but the carefree pleasurability of my life. I wanted them to want to be me. The deception was quite obviously that I had no intention whatsoever of giving myself to anyone.

Of course I had been seduced myself that night in the parking lot. It was not just that I wanted that convertible; I wanted to be that unknown but handsome and privileged young lover who owned it. Whose car it really was I never learned, but no matter, for in the next few months I became that unknown person, doing what I supposed he would be doing, even thinking his thoughts and adopting his values. It is not surprising then that, once seduced, I became seducer. How could I give myself to others when the person I wanted them to become was not even the person I was?

I was truly very seductive that summer. But because seduction has all the contradiction of desire within it, it fails if it succeeds—for we can never give what others want of us. Kierkegaard, for that reason, showed seduction to be a favorite hiding place of despair. Skillful seducers do not, like Don Juan, mindlessly exhaust themselves by making a large number of conquests, but plan elaborate ventures that hold one's interest and sustain one's anticipation as long as possible. Skillful seducers, in other words, engage directly in life as little as possible, looking forward to something which cannot in fact occur. The better they become at it, therefore, the emptier their lives become. So I lived as the unknown driver of that car, always anticipating what would never happen. I remained unknown to myself because I had shut my eyes inwardly, against my heart. The deeper begging I could not—or would not—hear.

Why then do we persist in desiring, and why do we not hear the genuine yearning of the heart for life? I am so impressed by the degree to which our lives are filled with the restless hunting and the empty seductiveness of desire that I am not at all sure I know the answer to this question. The answer I would suggest is a very simple one. The one apparent advantage of desire is that it focuses on objects and intends to take control of those objects. To desire something is to desire to *have* it. Most of us operate on the principle that to get what you want you must first acquire power sufficient to seize it. How common it is for children to be told that they will never have anything worth having until they have adequately educated or trained themselves—and to do so better than the others around them else they will get there too late or be too unprepared to take the prize. The element of control and power is important here, because it bears the implicit message that we cannot have what we desire until we are able to fashion a world that will provide it for us. It is a bid for divinity, an attempt to bring others into silent obedience. It is like being *peregrini* only on the condition that the sea and the weather submit to our commands. This, of course, is to live without venture, that is to say, without risk.

It should be clear by now that desiring is not only the opposite of prayer, it is the enemy of prayer. But this is not because, as the pious suggest, that it is a seeking after improper objects. It is the enemy of prayer because it is not seeking at all. It is, on the contrary, a subterfuge, a self-deception in which we need not deal with the open terror of genuine asking. By the exhausting pursuit of insatiable desire we need never face the possibility of growth, of asking for life in a way that makes birth possible. In the end the inherent contradictoriness of desire has the effect of canceling itself out as true desire. If we do not want the object, but only the wanting of it, we want nothing at all. If the ancient Romans had been consistent in their strategy for pleasure they would never have eaten, but would have spent their lives preparing to eat. And so it is with us, when we conceal our inner prayer under our preoccupation with desire, we do not live but only prepare to live.

We stand back from the table and snack with calculated restraint, refusing to accept the flesh and blood of true eucharistic passion.

But our preoccupation with desire is an unsuccessful strategy. The belief that we will one day find the object that will satisfy all our longing steadily loses its hold as we learn how unsatisfying satisfaction is. Finally, it is important to understand that the deeper restlessness that leaves us dissatisfied is the voice of the heart itself; it is the begging for life that does not want to show itself as a begging for life. Martin Heidegger once suggested that each of us has a complete poem somewhere within our soul. This inner poem is only partially expressed in what we say and write. In persons of great genius it emerges far more completely than in the rest of us, but in no one is it ever said in its entirety. Borrowing that charming metaphor, I would say that each of us has a prayer within, a genuine voice of the heart, but one we never express completely. In our restless desiring isolated syllables and even phrases of that beseeching voice can be heard. Desire is the prosaic effort to silence that voice with one or another object, to captain the heart, but the heart will not be quieted. It is inherently disobedient. But in this disobedience lies our truest hope.

The question before us in this meditation has been the proper response to God once we have been confronted by the immense silence of his listening. By *proper* here I do not mean correct. I mean it rather to have the sense of its Latin origin, *proprius*, one's own. How do I speak into the silence of expectation with my own voice? How do I allow the heart its disobedience in asking for what it wants?

The only proper response to God is to ask for that one thing we can truly receive, and which we can have only by receiving it—life itself. We can ask for nothing less if we truly ask. It is sometimes said that persons make the mistake in their praying of asking too much of God, that they bring before God the trivia of their daily preoccupations instead of focusing on one genuine issue—particularly on an issue which there is some reason to think God would want to resolve. I would suggest that it is otherwise, that we do not ask God for too much, but for far too little. And it is for this reason that we receive so very little. Asking for life is not asking for something reasonable; it is asking for everything miraculous.

But if we are to ask for everything, a new question emerges. What is it proper for God to give? What can God give that is God's alone to give? We can ask much of each other, but what we receive from each other is not properly God's—it is not only God's to provide. What then can God give us that no one else can give?

What God Can Properly Give

Speak to God from your heart. If you speak from your heart you will speak to God. And if you do speak to God you will ask for nothing less than life. But we close our eyes against our hearts, and instead of asking for life we pursue our desires for a different life, thereby asking for something we cannot have—because such asking is contradictory and therefore not asking at all.

There are good reasons for not asking, for denying the beggardom of the heart. For one thing, there are terrible risks involved in begging; in fact, risks we are sure to lose in matters of the spirit where gain is identical to loss. But there is a more powerful reason for not asking. There is only one thing more terrifying than losing—and that is receiving.

In this meditation we are concerned with what God gives in response to our asking. With what does God answer prayers? What does God offer and why is it so terrifying to open ourselves to it? So far I have left the issue rather abstract by saying it is *life* that we ask for. In this meditation I hope we can move from the abstract toward the concrete by way of giving substance to the anxiety necessarily involved in asking for life.

I begin by appealing to the simplest possible example: the

begging for life by infants. The most striking chracteristic of the pleading of babies is that they ask without first attempting to determine whether those who hear are those who are capable of responding. They do not even look first to see if there is anyone to hear them. In no way do they depend on their own ability to ascertain the reliable sources of life; they simply ask. They do not even *trust* those they ask. They ask first; it is only later that they learn some persons are more to be trusted than others.

We adults are not so careless, so desperate, so undefended as babies. We have learned that there are great differences between persons as to their resources, their availability, their talents, and their reliability. If babies reach out for life even before they have learned whom they can trust to respond, we reach out only after we have learned how far someone is to be trusted. We calculate our trust with great care, always concerned to reduce our risk, to cover our vulnerability,

But there is something elusive, perhaps even paradoxical in the nature of trust. We often attempt to arrange situations of trust in such a way that trust comes to resemble control. It is true, to be sure, that when I place my automobile in the hands of a mechanic, or my body in the hands of a surgeon, I trust them to do something for me that I cannot do for myself, and I certainly expect them to act in my self-interest even when I am not altogether sure what it is that constitutes my self-interest. But note carefully here that I have subtly hedged my trust. I make certain first that these persons are both competent to do the job to which I assign them, and that they are moreover good-willed toward me. Since they will in all likelihood do what I ask I am essentially in a position of power. I know before I go to them that they will do as I request. This may be what often goes by the name of trust, but it rather more strongly resembles obedience. However superior the mechanic and the surgeon may be to me in skill, they are nonetheless in my employ and therefore instruments of my

control. This kind of trust shuts off any true begging, and
stands at the opposite end of the spectrum from the child who
asks for life out of complete impotence.

I should add, though perhaps it is obvious, that trust of this
compromised sort is not found only in professional situations
where there is an exchange of money. It is even more common
in closer personal relations where we learn with each other
how much we can expect others to do for us on the basis of
pity, or guilt, or even love. I count on my friends, knowing that
they love me, to act on my behalf even when they occasionally
do so in ways that are painful to me.

What I am getting at here is that whenever we allow our
trusting relationships to be confused with power or control,
we have abandoned genuine, radical trust, and have ceased being suppliants with each other, acting as though we are actually sufficient in ourselves for all that we may need or want.
True trust has an altogether different quality to it. *I can trust
only those persons or powers over whom I have absolutely no
control.*

I am not recommending that we arrange our society so that
each person is encouraged to act without regard for anyone
else's expectations. Very quickly we would have no society at
all. There are degrees of societal influence and control that are
indispensible to life itself. As I have indicated in an earlier
meditation, we engage each other in a variety of contractual
arrangements that guarantee a sufficient social order—and to
do so requires that we live as suppliants with each other. I cannot make a payment of money to you unless you agree to accept it as money; I cannot have my children educated unless
there are those who respond to my pleas for a safe and
nourishing environment. We fulfill each other's expectations
in these matters far more than we usually realize. However—
and this is the critical point—if we *only* fulfilled each other's
expectations we would cease altogether to grow and develop

as complete human persons. We would have a society without variation; a society without a soul, like so many ants, or a colony of bacteria.

If we are dependent on each other for the order that makes life possible, we are even more dependent on each other for the kind of disorder that makes life human. But what sort of disorder am I speaking of? If I should have complete control over my social environment—that is, to fulfill all the popular ideals of adulthood—I should also lose all possibility of genuine dialogue with other persons; indeed, they would cease even to be *other* persons at all since they would all be but repetitions of myself. Therefore, what is needed is that others relate to me in ways that call from me resources and responses that I need to be human, but did not otherwise experience as needs at all.

Only when you come to me from outside the comfortable pattern of all my expectations can I act in ways that call for inner change and self-discovery on my part. I expected my wife, before we married, to be a loyal and uncritical supporter in all my professional and personal struggles. I expected my children to be dutiful, high achieving laborers toward the goals I have cherished most for myself. I expected blacks to be humbly grateful for their second great manumission in the sixties by white liberals like myself. I expected my students to have automatic respect for my erudition and to value the dispassionate pursuit of truth above all other ends. That none of these and similar expectations had the merest correspondence to the way these persons actually responded I now have to count as the most important sources of growth in my life. The experience of not getting what I wanted has been far more significant and shaping than the experience of getting what I wanted—not because I had to learn to settle for less than I had, but because I had to learn I could be so much more than I was.

Of course, no one is *made* to grow. Growth is always a choice. When my expectations are refused I do not have to respond by reaching to new resources within myself. I can hold out against those who have disappointed me, finding ways of repeatedly demanding that my sense of order, my priorities and values, be adhered to by others. I can turn inward with my resentments, disdainful of a world as disordered as this one. I may also adhere all the more closely to those forms of false trust where persons can be counted on to act in ways that favor my views and desires. I will design my political commitments by such a strategy, and limit my personal associations to those social bodies that resist the very kinds of disorder that trouble me. I can choose to grow by giving up an attempt to control those around me, or I can choose to stand fast, listening only to echoes of my own voice.

The description of radical trust I am offering does not, however, urge that we foster disorder merely for the sake of growth. The point is subtle, but it is crucial. If I intentionally spread chaos around myself, thereby forcing myself and others around me to act with greater resourcefulness, I am engaging only in another form of self-echoing. It is but a self-deceiving scheme of fulfilling my own expectations without appearing to do so. The deeper view here, the act of radical trust itself, can be stated finally only in paradoxical form: I must trust you to do something I cannot expect you to do; I must count on you to do what I cannot even imagine in prospect.

Note here that the emphasis is not on what you do; it is on my attitude toward what you do, my disposition toward the unfinished future. If I were courageous enough to expect you to do what I cannot expect, I will find that you will repeatedly offer the very challenges to my inwardness that make growth possible. If I am open to surprise, you will most certainly surprise me. If I genuinely trust you, I can expect you to do exactly what I do not want, but exactly what I need for growth. This is,

I believe, what Luther had in mind when he made his famous remark that God answers our prayers by refusing them.

I initiated this discussion of genuine, radical trust as a way of entering more deeply into the matter of asking from the heart. I observed at the beginning of this meditation that there are terrible risks involved in that kind of begging because what we are asking for is nothing less than life itself. What I then attempted to show is that what we ordinarily call trust is not trust at all, but a kind of control, a minimizing of risk. If we are really to trust another, it must be someone over whom we cannot exercise our will at all.

If the nature of radical trust is clear as I have described it, I hope it aids in focusing our attention on the very odd character of our trust in God. It is a trust that understands perfectly that God is least of all to be influenced by our intentions. In the case of God, as Luther's provocative remark suggests, we can expect only surprise. Turning toward God in the beggardom of our hearts we put all that we have and are under the greatest possible danger. For the greatest possible danger is not that we will lose our lives; it is rather that we will lose our lives for the sake of new life.

Assume for the moment that what I have been writing here is not a meditation but a dramatic piece. At the conclusion of the final point, imagine that the houselights go down and I quietly exit. The lights come up immediately on a sober gentleman dressed as a theologian. While he is evidently a rational and academic personage, the audience can detect some distress in his posture and tone of voice.

He begins by conceding to the audience that the discussion of trust they have just been entertained with has a good deal of superficial cleverness in it, and on its own terms is not to be controverted, but then he insists that it is a bald distortion of one of the grandest of theological doctrines. He pauses for a moment, then solemnly speaks the single word, "Grace."

Because the previous speaker has so emphasized the risk and danger of our relationship to God, calling on Luther's typically exaggerated remark for support, he overlooks the fact that with God all things are possible. Although God is God and beyond all possible human manipulation, God still does listen. It is a matter of the greatest religious truth, our theologian declares, his voice rising, that God is faithful to those who believe, and may be trusted to work toward the good in all things. And what is more, all that God does is done without the least expectation of a payment on the part of the faithful. This is precisely what the word, *grace*, means. The kind of talk we heard from the previous person on this stage weights the danger and risk of faith much too heavily, omitting the deep promise of the Gospel that God pours out a great abundance of life to those who ask.

The houselights go down, and I find myself back in the center of attention. Yes, I concede to the theologian, I did press very heavily on one side of this discussion, but, I then defend myself, only because everybody is already familiar with the other, and perhaps has even stopped to listen. When we say that with God all things are possible, we have the terrible habit of assuming this means that it is possible for God to do whatever we want. I wonder what our stage theologian thought at this point. Did he mean to say that it is possible for God to do whatever *we* want, or that it is possible for God to do whatever *God* wants. If the sober gentleman meant this remark in the former way it has the unfortunate consequence of silencing God, making the divine will dependent on our will. We become the captain, God the soldier. This is the reasoning of the turbaned brute within us.

The theologian could also have neutralized Luther's quotation by one of Paul's: If God is for us who can be against us? Here it does seem at first glance that God is offered as an ally who will strengthen us in the struggle with our enemies, guaranteeing victory in every instance. But to read it like this is to distort it, for the entire declaration hangs maddeningly from the first word: IF. This great IF stands between us and every statement we make about God's intentions. The IF demolishes any certainty we might have in the knowledge of God, and leaves all remarks permanently tentative.

I do not want to speak for our theatrical theologian, supposing that in his use of the word, grace, he has washed it clean of the mighty IF. He may very well know that to claim absolute freedom for God, is to invite this IF back into all our thoughts about and actions toward God. But I think I should say here that theologians have historically had a difficult time with the doctrine of absolute grace, for they could not easily admit that we have no influence whatsoever over this supremely free God.

In fact, I think it is useful here to take the next three paragraphs for a brief review of some of the elements in the theological struggle over the doctrine of grace. The doctrine is utterly simple when it has only to do with the freedom of God. Theologians have generally agreed that God is absolutely free, except where an act is illogical or contradictory. God cannot make something fall down and up at the same time, for example. The difficulties emerge when we try to include in the doctrine of grace the possibility that God might also do what we want God to do. In its strongest form God appears quite indifferent to our wishes. There must be a way the doctrine can be modified to eliminate divine indifference. Medieval theologians in particular became extremely clever in cutting away at the harshness of the doctrine of absolute grace. While never abandoning the fundamental claim that God alone can save us, they did teach in a variety of ways that God cares whether we care to be saved. It does not seem reasonable to say that God will save those who openly resist salvation, and in their hearts detest God. It would follow then that the first movement in grace is not God's but ours; we must first move toward God from the heart, then God will respond. God will wait until we first do what it is possible for us to do within ourselves (*facere quod in se est*) even if that action is exceedingly modest in scope.

While this may be a most reasonable modification of absolute grace, it nonetheless radically altered the nature of the relationship between the human and the divine. It is true that it has the effect of making God responsive to us, and not merely reckless in absolute indifference; it makes God a listener. But at the same time this modification insists that God also remain powerful, and that God's power be responsive to our will to the degree that a genuine movement of the heart toward God would not be refused. In this sense God's listening takes the form of obedience—the obedience of a trusted ally. The silence of God is now an imposed silence, no longer the silence of expectation.

This compromise in the doctrine of grace was serious enough that it gave rise to the Protestant Reformation. Luther, following the teaching of Augustine more than a thousand years earlier, insisted that there was no way God's absolute freedom could be compromised without making God less than God. Augustine had said that grace was "prevenient," that is, it comes before all else. It comes before even the heart's movement toward God. Luther agreed. "Let God be God," he demanded. But he was also concerned that we not think in consequence that God need not therefore be concerned with the longing of the human heart. Strongly influenced by the biblical picture of Christ, Luther taught that God does not come to us in glory, but in suffering. We do not assemble before the heavenly throne as the mute auditors of God's imperative word, but stand at the foot of the cross where God is present in perfect silence. Luther did not compromise God's absolute grace in the least; he presented it rather as a grace of expectation rather than a grace of power. God comes to us first as a listener, not a speaker. God does not come when we call; God is there, then we call.

If grace is understood in this Augustinian and Lutheran

way, we can see more completely how it is related to the kind of radical trust I discussed earlier. To let God be God is to take leave of any thought that we can have an influence on the divine will. Even if we are certain that God loves us, we can have no certainty whatsoever how this love will express itself, or even that we can recognize it as love. To put it another way, the certainty that God loves us must always contain within itself the great divine IF. The faithful know they are in the hands of God, but they also know they have no hand of their own on God.

I must concede that by emphasizing that our trust in God must be a radical trust that takes the divine IF into itself, I have made the silence of God even more formidable. God seems more and more remote. There is nothing recognizable in the divine mind, no pattern of actions we can depend on. It is one thing to say that God's silence is the silence of listening, but it is quite another to say that we can actually speak to a God so silent we can know nothing about divine reality, a God whose mind remains a complete cipher. How do we speak to someone we do not know, whom we cannot see or hear, who never speaks back at the other end of the phone? What is worse, when Christians insist that this is a God who listens, they do so on the basis that God became one of us, living our life and dying our death. But this is a harsh teaching. It is almost like saying that God not only does not speak back but that he hung up the phone 2,000 years ago.

For all I know, our imagined theologian may be embarrassed by this latter difficulty, for it may be that he, too, was puzzled as a child when his grandmother instructed him simply to close his eyes and speak to God from his heart. He is embarrassed because the adult he wanted to become would have understood these matters. Now he discovers that the adult he did become is still the child he was. He remains a beginner in the question of prayer.

But we should not be impatient with him, because we can understand that the question he is now pondering is one of great weight, even for adults. It is certainly the most important question to be discussed in this meditation; indeed, in all of these meditations. Let me try, then, to state it as clearly as possible.

How can we speak to someone when it is impossible to know what they have heard us say, or whether they have heard us at all? When we speak with each other it seems as though we have a rather clear idea to whom we are speaking and how they therefore happen to hear it. We do after all share a language, and generally have enough experience in common that our minds are not ciphers to each other. Within a tolerable margin of error I can assume that you will understand what I am saying in the same way that I understand it.

While this seems to be a reasonable account of our use of language with each other, it hides a fatal contradiction within itself. To state the contradiction in its most pungent form, *If I know exactly what you understand when I speak to you, it is not you to whom I am speaking; I am speaking to myself.* It is certainly true that in most every instance we speak on the assumption that those who hear us will understand what we are saying in the same way we do. But take note of the implications in this assumption. It would seem that I have no reason to speak to you at all unless I knew that what I wish to say you do not yet know, or do not yet understand. Therefore my purpose for speaking is to eliminate the differences between us; to render your mind identical to mine, even an extension of mine. This, oddly, has the effect of bringing speech to an end. Once you have been properly informed, neither of us has further need to speak—unless, of course, it develops that there is another matter in which you need to be informed and silenced.

The assumption that I can know what you hear when I speak to you can only lead to the silence of obedience. This is a circumstance no different in principle from speaking to a computer capable of repeating all that we have said quite as we have said it. It may appear for a while, particularly if the computer is very sophisticated, that I am having a kind of conversation with it. I am giving it instructions, and it is responding very much as attentive and obedient students might, achieving facility with technical and difficult words and seizing hold of the basic thought patterns. What will become evident shortly is that this is not a conversation at all, for the reason that the computer can say nothing back to me which I do not already understand—which, in fact, I have not already said myself. I am not talking with the computer, therefore, but with myself; and, since in talking with myself I already know what I am about to say, I have no reason to say it, and therefore cease talking altogether.

Indeed, strange and even paradoxical as it sounds, *I can talk with you only if I do not know in advance what you understand when I speak*, only when I cannot know in advance what you will do with my words. In genuine conversation we speak words and sentences to each other over which we have abandoned all control. In fact, I do not even know what I have said until I learn what you have done with what I have said. The most creative conversation will therefore occur only where persons address those areas in each other most completely unknown to the speaker—creative because then each response must be a kind of surprise for the speaker, a discovery of something that could not otherwise have been known. This is really no different from saying that creative conversation occurs when people speak to each other as though they were truly listening to, and not simply recording, what the other is saying. In other words, if you are listening to me it is *you* listening, and it is *you* who respond. You are not responding according to my signals as though I had you programmed. If I can control what you hear or how you respond, it is no longer you listening.

The question is, how can we speak to persons whose minds are a cipher to us? The answer is that we can speak to persons only to the degree that their minds are a cipher. The most important implication of this answer is that if I cannot close your mind to the shape and content I desire it to have I must keep my own mind open to your response. The reason this is so very important is that keeping myself open to your response is indispensable to life itself. When I can no longer respond to you, or to anyone else, I am effectively dead. My inability to know in advance what you will do in response to my words and actions is not a hindrance to the smooth operation of my life, but an invitation to increasing growth and vitality. This also means, of course, that every overture to you, every word, entails something of a risk, a letting go of my control over the situation. It is a willingness, in other words, to listen. Genuine conversation implies a relationship of radical trust as I have described it.

It should be apparent that I am appealing here to the distinction made in the first meditation between the kinds of speaking that correspond to the silence of obedience and the silence of expectation. These two ways of describing language are by no means original with this meditation. They are taken from two classical theories of language, one that has its first significant expression in Plato, and one most fully stated in the work of Wittgenstein in the present century. I shall integrate these theories into the discussion by referring to the *theatrical* and the *dramatic* uses of language—terms not borrowed from the philosophers but adapted playfully from the motif of this meditation.

When we speak theatrically we have already determined what the auditors, or audience, are to hear. We deliver our speech as though it were script. It is the case, to be sure, that actors do not know their audience personally, and are therefore speaking to hidden minds. The audience is silent; it is listening. However, it is also the case that the art of acting requires one to take the side of the audience—that is, to be one's own audience, both speaking and observing oneself as the speaker. Indeed this is precisely what acting is. For this reason it does not matter *which* persons are in the theater, or even if anyone is there at all. The cast may perform brilliantly in dress rehearsal to empty seats, or even in their private dressing rooms, speaking their lines into the mirror. Their success as performers depends on the degree to which the audience can allow themselves to be represented in the actors' self-observation—not only to speak for them, but also to listen for them.

When we speak dramatically we relinquish all control over our words, and therefore cannot know in advance how they will be received. We cannot observe ourselves in dramatic speech, as though we are our own listeners, for we cannot know how we are being heard or what the hearers will do with what we are saying. Nor do those to whom we truly speak understand themselves to be placed before us as audience. As they listen to us they are also preparing to respond. The audience of theatrical speech does not respond to the performers, except to applaud or hiss, indicating how masterfully the cast has responded to each other in the place of the audience. Naturally, once the audience believes they are being addressed by the actors, they would cease being audience and would cry out to Oedipus that he is unknowingly courting his own mother. Were this to happen we could only consider it a theatrical failure.

Some years ago, near the beginning of that period when the theater of the absurd came to dominate the off-Broadway stage in New York, my wife and I, both quite taken with that particular fashion of playwrighting and acting, attended a play given in a tiny theater by a group unknown to us. As it happened, there were only two actors—also unknown to us—performing all the roles of the play. The energy of the two players, a man and a woman, was phenomenal. They were not on the stage five minutes before they became involved in a passionate, fast-paced verbal confrontation with each other that had all the theatrical signs of physical threat. They were wonderfully inventive in the irrationality of their exchanges. In spite of the fact that it was not possible to make the least sense of their altercation, it felt remarkably real. I still remember the excitement of it, even if I never found the thread of their menacing discourse.

But then something happened that disturbs me to this day. The actress suddenly broke away and came downstage toward the audience, while the actor sustained his verbal barrage with scarcely a pause. The actress, speaking directly to the audience in a subdued but intense voice, said, "Ladies and gentlemen, I am distressed to tell you that this man is having a nervous breakdown. He has lost all capacity for rational action, and I am afraid something violent will happen, either to me or to you. Therefore, I ask you, please leave the theater."

The audience sat transfixed. The actress searched our faces in apparent desperation. A brilliant performance, without question. "Please, I beg you, leave the theater. This is not part of the script. This man is dangerous. For your own safety, leave at once."

Embarrassed glances were shared throughout the house. The actor continued to rave, unaffected by the woman's remarks. But no one moved. One person began vigorously to applaud, but stopped when the actress held up a hand. She repeated her plea. Here and there the audience began to stir. I looked at my wife to see her reaction. Without a word she rose and started walking out. Someone followed her. I began to worry that the actress would lose her audience, hesitated but then followed my wife. "Listen to me. Please, listen," she pleaded.

We all left. But not one member of that audience reached the street certain they should be there. In fact, no one spoke. Each of us made our separate way into the night. I take it that the play closed shortly after that, for I never saw another notice for it and, since it was a modest production to begin with, it was never reviewed.

To this day I do not know whether the actress was speaking theatrically or dramatically. I do not know if her words were script or address. Was she really asking us to leave, or was she acting out her request? Did she observe herself so carefully as to know how her words were being received, or was she putting herself in our hands? Were we audience or listeners? Could she have done this same scene in rehearsal before an empty house?

What is disturbing about this experience is not the danger the audience or the actress might have been in, but the impossibility to tell whether it was a theatrical or a dramatic event. The question disturbs because ordinarily we have no difficulty distinguishing between a theatrical and a dramatic gesture. There are many occasions in the lives of all of us when we intend to communicate a certain meaning to others, altogether unconfused about the effect toward which we are aiming. On those occasions we employ every acting technique we possess. If we become skillful enough we may even act as though we had convinced ourselves. That actress showed every sign of believing her words. Of course, what we do know is that if she was acting she did not believe what she was saying. Neither do we believe ourselves when we endeavor to direct the responses of our assorted audiences according to our script. There is no question that the actress knew, regardless of our perception of what she was doing.

Consider now the implications of the theatrical and dramatic uses of language in our relation to God. There is no doubt that we can approach God theatrically, having in mind a clear script for both speaker and listener. In this case God becomes audience, a passive and obedient presence, an extension of our own will and mind. In the theatrical relationship God becomes thoroughly trustworthy—but also ceases to be

God. Whenever we presume to know the mind of God sufficiently to know how we are being heard, God is no longer God, and we are no longer listened to. All of our praying is in this instance just so much dress rehearsal. If we are not listened to, we are not truly speaking but only voicing sounds into empty space. And if we are not speaking we are isolated and closed into ourselves, slowly suffocating in our own exhalation.

The same point applies to God. If God were to conduct all affairs theatrically it would be in the mode of grand display. God would have become impresario of the universe, performing it for some audience unknown to us, or perhaps rehearsing it before an empty house. If God is to relate to us meaningfully through the spoken word it is necessary that God be at risk quite as any other speaker. God must speak, and then be silent, waiting to see what is done with those words by listeners. But the risk for God must be a genuine risk; there must be a willingness to lose the status of God. And this is precisely what happens according to the gospel: God emptied of divinity, living in our midst and at our mercy. The gospel is the declaration that God has given up all forms of theatricality, and has become dramatic, leaving the future radically open.

Now the question to which this meditation is addressed confronts us in a new way. I have tried to show that there is something analogous between our speaking to God and our speaking to each other. It is not only God who must remain unknowable to the speaker—it is any listener whosoever. So the question before us is whether there is a fundamental difference between the way God listens to us and the way others listen to us. *What does God say that no one else can say?*

What we can know for certain here is that our listening to each other will always be incomplete. No matter how silently we present ourselves to each other, it is always the case that we will be listening *for* something in what anyone is saying. We are limited by the fact that we share a world with the speaker.

By "world" here I mean an intelligible pattern of expectations. If you should suddenly yell, "Watch out!", I can be counted on to jump out of the way, or turn quickly to see what is coming. You can anticipate to a large degree how I will respond to your words and actions—and I can know with some confidence what you expect me to do. I can share a world with you only when there is a limit to the amount of surprise in our responses to each other. If every action is a surprise, I literally have no world to live in with you. A world become unpredictable has ceased being a world. To say that we have become unpredictable to each other is to say that because we do not share a language, and a great many other cultural customs, what we do is unintelligible to each other. In that case, we do not share a world.

I observed above that in every family there is a fabric of trust that allows each member to know how the others are likely to respond to them. It is such trust, shared by a large number of persons, that makes a world possible.

In fact, each of us lives in a number of worlds, defined in this way. And some of the persons we share one world with may be helplessly lost and alien in another of our worlds, or simply out of place and uncomfortable. A former president of my university came from the world of business. Having been a shrewd and accomplished business executive he was unashamed to talk to students and faculty in the way he would have addressed his employees, apparently unaware he was now in a different world. He was, therefore, widely distrusted in the university, and distrusted by the very persons who admired his genius at commerce. In private conversation with him I was astounded to discover how well he could listen. It was obvious he knew he was in a different world, and one whose pattern of expectations he had still to learn. He had the habit, however, of concluding his discussions as though he were adjourning a meeting of his staff. I had the feeling at those moments that he thought it was the responsibility of professors to turn a profit for the university. I cannot help but think he was aware of his movement from world to world, but that he frankly preferred the world of commerce. He soon returned to that preferred world and with obvious enthusiasm, but not before bringing the university to unprecedented financial health.

When we speak to each other it is always within the context of one or another world, and therefore it is according to the expectations inherent in that world that we listen to what is said. That is why I do not simply listen to what you are saying, but listen *for something* that you are saying. I am listening to find out how I should respond to you within the world that we share. When the university president spoke as a chief executive officer I heard little that I expected to hear, and therefore did not know how to respond.

We should take special note here of a peculiar characteristic of a "world" as I have spoken about it: the reason that our listening is always incomplete is that the world in which we speak precedes our speaking into it. We speak and listen in terms of an already existing world—or so we usually understand it. Our businessman president understood that we had an established world whose ways he had not learned. This seems to give the world considerable power, for it would appear that we are shaped by the worlds in which we live and move.

Another way to say this is that we are never completely silent with each other. We never live in purely dramatic terms. When you begin to speak I may be vocalizing nothing, and be silent in that sense, but I am attempting to identify a script— even if it is a very loose one—by which I will know how to reply; that is, reply in a way that is intelligible to you even if you had not expected me to reply with exactly these words.

Observe now how important it is that God's silence is complete, that God does not belong to anyone's world and is not to be managed to any degree by an existing script. Our relationship to God cannot therefore be theatrical in any sense but must always be dramatic. That is, the fact that we cannot know God means that we cannot ever completely prepare ourselves against surprise. We cannot know for certain the meaning of our discourse with each other. *Because of the dramatic silence of God there is nothing necessary about our worlds*. The network of trust that gives it what permanence it has can vanish in an instant. No one needs to be convinced how suddenly it is possible for societies, families, friendships to pass from order to chaos.

The completeness of God's silence is such that we never encounter that silence *within* a world. A world is a world only so far as we can anticipate each other's responses; since we cannot anticipate God's response under any circumstance there is no way we can give God's silence a worldly shape. We cannot say, in other words, what God is being silent about—as though if God were to speak we would know exactly what would be said. (We sometimes make a remark like, "If your mother were still alive, I know exactly what she would say about this." We know, that is, what she is silent about, even when it is death that has silenced her.) As I noted in the first meditation, any attempt to translate God's silence into speech in any form can produce nothing more than a worldly voice masquerading as a divine voice.

If it is not within the world that we encounter the silence of God, then where is it? *It is God's silence that touches us whenever we see our worlds as possible worlds*, whenever we are aware that there is always something behind a world that cannot be trusted. The silence of God has touched us when we know that we can have our worlds only as we are able to beg each of those with whom we share our worlds to continue in them. We come upon the silence of God each time we step to the stagelights to explain how things really are—and know inside ourselves that we have not addressed our listeners but recited script to our audience, a script we do not believe ourselves. It is the silence of God that causes us genuinely to implore, "Listen to us, please." As long as we continue in our worldly roles, careful to find the stagelight, we will only speak *about something* and never *to someone*.

Perhaps I am giving the impression that I understand the silence of God to be a largely negative, decaying influence on human affairs, ultimately destructive of all our worlds. I may seem to represent God's silence as little different from time itself as it wears away all human resolve, returning civilizations to the wilderness, art to dust. If so, I have obscured the splendid fact that it is God's unintelligibility, God's final and irreducible silence, that shines through all the manifold imperfections of our worlds—repeatedly offering us the possibility of the gift of authentic humanness. Indeed, the more predictable and rational a world is the more it suffocates true discourse between persons, and the less possible it is to speak to each other from the heart. In a family where everyone has a clear part and adheres consistently to an order all the others observe, we may be certain that the wishes of the heart are not known to each other. It is not that God destroys human culture by way of silence, but that human culture consistently turns against itself in its attempt to speak for God. It is only in situations rich with surprise, only when life is filled with grace, that we can speak with each other meaningfully.

In other words, something miraculous is occurring here. If the world's voices were the voice of God, then we could not speak to one another at all. If a world were to be so permanent as to be utterly predictable—with a flawless script—we could do no more than serve as each other's audience, which is no different from being faithful recorders, sophisticated computers that operate on a mutually compatible program. We would cease to be human. It is for this reason that all of the great religions have been so watchful against idolatry, or the worship of false gods—which in our terms is confusing the voices of the world with the silence of the holy. In every form of tyranny, in every attempt to silence others into obedience, there is an inherent idolatry. The miracle of grace is that there is a deeper, profounder silence that rots out the feet of all our idols, and because it is a silence that no speech can exhaust it is a silence that makes all speech possible.

But there is more to the miracle. The silence of God has the effect of revealing over and over again the ultimate theatricality of our worlds. If a world consists of the predictable responses we make to each other's words and actions it is evident that we must know the script *before* we can share that world. This means that the strong sense that the world precedes our speaking with each other is false. There is no world until we speak it with each other. Far from being shaped by our worlds, we are, jointly, the creators of all of them. To understand ourselves as their creatures is the very soul of idolatry. It is true that when you speak to me you already have a relatively clear idea of a proper response, and it may seem that for that reason the world precedes my response, but, in fact, if I do not respond as you expect, your world becomes mute and impotent. Our businessman-president's initial refusal to acknowledge the academic script led to our distrust —not because we thought he would remain an impotent outsider, but because we feared the loss of our own world and the resulting powerlessness. We were idolaters fearing exposure.

So far I have discussed theatricality in sharply negative terms. I want now to emphasize precisely the opposite. Theatricality can also be irrepressibly joyous—but only when it disavows its idolatrous character and openly disbelieves in the worlds it creates. Stage performers exercise maximum skill in persuading us of the reality of their presentation. They intend to be perfectly believable, and to have exclusive control of the audience's attention. *However*, they do so while simultaneously making it quite clear that they are pretending it all. It is a ruse, but a ruse that advertises itself as such. It is the strictest possible divination of a world, convincing every listener that the pattern of expectations could not vary in the least detail—but it is an idolatry that lifts its skirts through the whole proceeding, leaving its clay feet in such plain view that the most rapt audience cannot forget for a second they are in the theater. Audiences seem to forget—but they only *seem* to. How often does it happen in a theater or movie house that, even in the most absorbing presentation, persons act as if they were participants in the depicted events? I have never seen, nor heard of, a member of the audience rushing to the stage to prevent a tragedy, or to join in the fun.

The joyousness of the theatrical is evident even in its terminology. We call a stage piece a *play*. No matter how serious the subject matter it is still a play, and as such by no means serious. It is one thing for Aufidius to murder his beloved rival, Coriolanus, in an ambivalent explosion of passion; it is quite another for this tragedy to be enacted before the lights. The more deeply we feel the pain of this ironic act—the terrible sense of loss experienced by the murderer—the more likely we will be on our feet seconds later at the conclusion of the play with bravos for the performers. It is a human misfortune we can rejoice over. Great theater is thoroughly celebratory.

All art, indeed all creative activity, has the quality of theatricality, or playfulness. I should even say *self-declared* playfulness. The artistic impulse is not at bottom political; it does not intend to change the world. It is far more fundamental and radical than that, for what it intends is the creation of a pretend world. It offers us new patterns of expectation. The artist does not show us the truth about the world, but shows us a way of looking and listening that makes a new world possible.

The highest achievement of the arts in this respect is not bringing into actual existence one of these possible worlds, but bringing us to see that all our worlds are possible worlds. Doubtless, one of the reasons so many artists have suffered exile, imprisonment, and even death in totalitarian societies, and continue to do so, is that rulers cannot allow the people to see that the structure of their society is not necessary but only

possible. Playfulness is dangerously infectious. When artists
so baldly announce their idolatry we are likely to discover our
own. We may realize that our society is actually a play society,
that if we do not continue to perform it, it will cease at once to
exist. This is an extension of the point made earlier, that no
matter how clearly defined your world may be, if I do not respond according to your expectations it becomes mute and
impotent. We can put it a bit more playfully by saying that if
we do not rise in the morning and decide at once to perform
our university with each other, or our corporation, or our
neighborhood, there simply will be none. This is true for every
human institution, even the family. If family members do not
play their respective roles, performing the parts of parents
and children, it will simply not be a family.

There are, to be sure, limits to the degree of theatricality we
can tolerate in our lives. Even if we can see how we play at
business, or education, or family, can we say the same for
poverty, or disease, or warfare? Do persons perform cancer, or
ignorance? These seem brutally real and, as such, absolute
barriers to joyousness. We may celebrate an actor's stage
death; can we celebrate his real death? The question before us
concerns the depth of theatricality, and the claim that all our
worlds are play worlds. We are confronted now with the view
that in the end all playing is playing around, and eventually
must yield to reality, like childhood must yield to adulthood,
or vacations yield to work schedules. This was fun, we say, but
now back to the real world; it is now time to get serious. No
matter how wonderful the actors have been, they must eat,
after all, and pay their rent.

Religiously speaking, however, even the reality we turn back
to when we have finished our play is but another kind of play.
The only difference is that when we get back to work we attempt to convince ourselves that work is something necessary
and refuse to see it as an activity we choose creatively to do.
Theologians have a surprising way of talking about this. They

refer to God as the Creator. "God never ceases from making
something or other," wrote Philo Judaeus, a first-century
Jewish thinker. "As it is the property of fire to burn, and of
snow to chill, so also it is the property of God to be creating."
This is a description of God as an artist, as a dramaturge com-
posing the universe for no other reason than the joy of doing
it. Christians add to this doctrine, by way of the Incarnation,
the notion that God plays a part in this drama by taking a
human role in human history.

Earlier I made a distinction between the dramatic and the
theatrical—giving obvious preference to the dramatic. I defined the dramatic situation as one in which we do not proceed
with each other by way of a script, but are genuinely open to
the future. It should now be clear that the dramatic is not absolutely antithetical to the theatrical, but takes the theatrical
into itself. That is, when the theatrical affirms itself as the
theatrical, it sets its scripts aside as only possible scripts and
opens forward to an unpredictable future. You relate to me
dramatically when you plainly show that you are approaching
by way of a script, but a script that will be changed by my
response. Your life has a shape given it by both circumstance
and design, but it is a shape that anticipates changes that cannot be predicted in advance. You come to me out of a world,
but you do not require me to respond to it in precisely its own
terms. Let us have a new world together, you say to me.

This is simply a way of saying that life never comes without
a context. We do not live our lives as isolated individuals. It is
not some organic current that energizes our various parts.
Life is always life together; it is a way of being with others; it
is always received by way of being given, and never is there
receiving without giving.

Our resistance to God, our idolatrous desire to speak for
God, instead of to God, when faced with this immense silence,
is a resistance to the unceasing divine creativity. We want to
appeal to God out of the context of our world. We want God to

improve it, somehow to amend it in our favor. This is precisely why we ask God for far too little. We do not ask for life, but for a different life—in terms of our present world. But in giving what God alone can give, God gives much more than this. In answering our prayers, *God does not respond within a world; God responds with a world*.

When we pray to a Creator we can only ask for that which will begin now, which will be original and therefore unforeseen. It is asking to be surprised. This has a remarkable consequence. It means that whatever happens to us is the beginning of something that never before existed. It is an opening forward into the unknown. All our existing forms of knowledge are always according to one world or another. Such knowledge depends on looking backward, establishing continuities, showing the inherent lawfulness of events. Knowledge that comes from within a world in this careful way has the potential of explaining everything that occurs in that world—but cannot explain the world itself. To acknowledge that God's response to us is the creation of a world is to acknowledge the ultimate mysteriousness of that world. When we respond to each other from within the context of our world, it has the effect of making that world intelligible. When God responds with a world, its intelligibility is transformed into mystery. We no longer merely understand our world, but are astounded by it, by the fact that there is a world at all. It is an occasion for the grandest of all bravos.

But now we are faced with the most difficult question of all. If God gives us nothing less than the world, how can we possibly receive it?

What We Can Properly Receive From God

As I suggested in the second meditation, the classical form of prayer is that of the father of the epileptic in the Gospel of Mark: "I believe, help my unbelief." The emphasis in this prayer is not on belief, but on help. Believing and asking for help are radically different activities. In declaring our beliefs we talk about something, in crying out for help we speak to someone.

I might as well admit now what some readers have no doubt already perceived: that the distinction between *talking about* and *speaking to* is essentially false. Finally, all language is spoken to someone; it is always address. The distinction between these two modes is not found, therefore, in language itself but in the way we use language. We often speak as though we are talking about something, and even suppose that our talk is authenticated by that to which it refers. That is, if I am not talking about something I am not really talking, just making sounds. This is a mistaken view of language, in my judgment, and I have been assuming an opposite view from the beginning: *if you are not speaking to someone you are not speaking at all.*

It is in the fact that all speech is address that its religious possibilities lie. All speech, in other words, is a form of prayer.

Whatever else we may be saying each time we address another, we are beseeching them, "Listen to me. Please, listen." Our very lives depend on that listening. This plea is not merely one of the things we utter in our speech, it is what we utter with the whole of our speech. We never speak except to be heard. When we are not heard we have not truly spoken. And when we cannot speak we have increasingly less to say, therefore less to ask for, and the lights of our being steadily darken.

But for all this we nonetheless have a deep and powerful resistance to prayer. We do not want to hear that voice in our speech, petitioning for selfhood. It is, of course, terrifying to know how completely we depend on others merely to *be* at all. We hide that terror by attempting to silence others, to give our speech a power that can arrange our world as we desire to have it. If we can use language to create a world dependent on us, we need not acknowledge the depth of our dependence on each other. This use of language is the very inversion of all that is religious; it is the basis for every form of idolatry.

The religious possibilities of language are realized when we find ourselves being searched by the silence of another, and are thereby freed to say what we want to say, and to say what we want. Earlier I commented that although this kind of listening is powerless, inasmuch as it cannot arrange the world into a desired order, it is creative—and creative in a strong sense of that word. That is, a creative listener is not someone who simply allows me to say what I already want to say, but someone whose listening actually makes it possible for me to say what I never could have said, and thus to be a new kind of person, one I have never been before and could not have been before this directed listening. It is such a continuing re-creation of selfhood that occurs in genuinely dramatic discourse, and never at all in purely theatrical discourse.

In the previous meditation I stressed the fact that no matter how well we listen to each other, our listening will always be partial. We listen to each other from out of the world we share.

We are never completely silent for each other. One world or another will always be insinuating its script into our conversations. For that reason our existence in each world is always a partial existence; there is always something left out, something to say which cannot be heard there. Thus the importance of the silence of God, a silence that does not come to us in the shape of a world. The question in the third meditation had to do with what God could give us by way of that silence. As we saw, it makes no sense to say that God answers us in terms of the world from which we have uttered our petitions. For in that case God's answer would be indistinguishable from the world's answer—with the consequence that we either discount the power of God or idolize the power of the world. God does not answer within the world, but with the world. God does not rearrange the world so as to present us with that one priceless object that satisfies all our desires. God does nothing less than give us the world itself.

I noted before that one of the problems of prayer is not that we ask for too much, but for too little. Now we have come to another problem: God does not answer with too little, but with too much. The question before us now is how we can receive what God has given us, and receive it in a way that does not violate the limitations of our humanity.

In other words, how do we receive the world and remain human? Kierkegaard addressed this problem in his brief but extraordinary book *The Philosophical Fragments*. He was reflecting on the difficulty God is under in expressing love for human beings. Kierkegaard animates the dilemma by putting it in the form of a fairy tale in which a great king has fallen in love with a peasant girl. Being a king, he has unlimited resources available in his wooing of the girl. He could surround her with gifts of inestimable value, summon before her matchless spectacles and entertainments, even bring her into court with all its splendor in full display. He could, in short, set the world at her feet. But at the same time, the king knows

that to do so could only confuse her. It would be such a meaningless change from everything with which she was familiar,
that she would no longer know who she was, and perhaps even
cease being the person the great king loved.

How can we receive the world without ceasing to be the persons God has given it to?

I want to continue in my meditation on this question by di-
viding it into two parts: How much life can we receive? How
can we live as the receivers of this much life?

How much life can we receive from the God who wants to
give us nothing less than the world?

I find it significant that what brings people to prayer with
the greatest urgency is a threat to their lives, or a threat to the
life of someone they love. Even if you have never truly prayed
in your lifetime, you may drop to your knees without the least
hesitation when suddenly faced with the imminent possibility
of your death, or the death of your child. I am writing this
meditation less than a week after the subject of prayer became a news item of considerable fascination—and for this
very reason. An American general was abducted by Italian terrorists. There was little hope of his safe return, and his family,
in addition to public appeals to the terrorists, asked the world
to join them in their prayers. When the Italian police learned
of the terrorists' hiding place and daringly stormed it without
loss of life, the American general himself thanked the world
for their prayers, without which, he was certain, he could not
have been freed.

The question here is not whether God arranged to have the
police carry out their mission successfully—having first been
moved by the prayers of the general's family and friends. It is
not difficult to imagine that the terrorists themselves saw
their mission as something of a holy cause and were avidly
praying for its success, and for the lives of those many persons
they supposed this general could have taken with his enor-

mous army. When we put the question this way it suggests that the general's side won their appeal to God by outnumbering their opponents, or having a cause that was dearer to God's heart. But this is a skewed way of putting the question. I am sure that there was much prayer around this event, and that much of it was a genuine begging for life. The question now is how much life each of these beseeching hearts was able to receive.

We are tempted here to think that once the general was freed the need for prayer had passed. In fact, that need now becomes more acute. Having been offered life, can the general now pray to receive it? That is the real question of the efficacy of prayer

What is implied is that it is possible for us to beg for life in ways that do not prepare us to receive life. This happens when we do not pray for life as such, but pray *against death*. The prayer for life in this case was a prayer for a longer life—indeed, at core it was a petition for unending life. Such a prayer is so characteristic of religious persons that belief in God is widely associated with belief in immortality. I frequently hear people say that they are not religious, or that they do not sympathize with religion of any kind, because they do not believe in life after death. My students are commonly astonished to learn that some religions have no interest at all in surviving death, and sometimes teach that continuing to exist after death is an appalling spiritual disaster. Is the prayer against death, the prayer for unending life, actually a prayer for life itself?

Some fifteen years ago I spent two unforgettably pleasant summers with my wife and three children in a camp and conference center in Wisconsin, where I served as a staff member. It was a colorful—and at times almost zany—place, that attracted groups of the most varied character. There was a high school cheer-leading training session; there were conventions of banjo players, karate instructors, trampoline performers, workshops for conservation groups, volleyball coaches, and first-aid teachers; and even quiet periods restricted to retired YM-YWCA executives.

What I remember most vividly, however, is a group far less conspicuous than all of these, but far more unusual than any group I had ever met. There were perhaps thirty persons in this group. They were all middle-aged or older, and most of them, I suspect, were retired. It was evident that they had all been more or less successful in worldly terms. I noticed first that they were unusually friendly and high-spirited; indeed, they were consistently, uninterruptedly cheerful. What made them unique as a group, however, was not their happy disposition. It was that each person or couple had lost a loved one, and in their grief had consulted a famous English medium, drawn by her famous ability to establish contact with the dead.

The English medium, or "sensitive" as they preferred to call her, undoubtedly possessed considerable psychic powers, for she was able to produce a large amount of very personal information about each of the dead loved ones. Her method was described by several persons in the group. She had a contact in the spirit world, a being she referred to as an "excarnate," or someone who had once lived in the flesh as we do (there are also "discarnates," apparently, who have never incarnated), but whom she had never known on this side. The contact, in fact, had lived in an earlier century, the seventeenth I think, and was performing this service as a kind of penance for an ill-spent life. At the sensitive's request the contact would pass communications back and forth between the dead and their living loved ones.

In the course of time, each of these people became quite attached to the English sensitive, and it was through her that they became acquainted with each other. The contact had died some ten years before that summer, leaving her clients suddenly without any means of staying in touch with their own excarnates. Their understandable reaction was to draw themselves into an intimate circle in the hope that they might by a special collective effort acquire some of the sensitive's powers, or that the sensitive herself might establish contact with them. Their effort was deeply rewarding, for by one means or another they were able to continue gathering personal data from the other side. It had become their custom to gather once each year at this camp in Wisconsin, coming from wherever their homes might be.

I became quite friendly with one couple in particular in this group. They were both retired professionals, in their late seventies, vigorously alert, and happy to talk at length about their experiences. In his second year of medical school their son, an only child, was in an automobile accident that "excarnated" both him and his dog. After a terrible period of suffering—a suffering, they now knew, that had come from mistaking the true nature of death—they had been directed to the English sensitive. They had spent considerable time in her home attempting to reach their son. Their efforts were more successful than they could have imagined, for the boy was not only alive in the other world, but was happier than he had ever been on this side. This was remarkable, because, his parents reported, he had always seemed a happy lad. When I asked them why they were so sure that it was their son with whom the sensitive was in communication, they responded with laughter and, both speaking at once, told me what was for them the most convincing and touching detail: their son's dog was with him, a dog accurately named and described by the sensitive, even though, separated by an ocean, she could never possibly have seen.

I want to stress the fact that this was an apparently normal and successful couple. There was nothing bizarre about them, and they were manifestly happy. I did notice, however, that all references to their son were in the present tense. One would have thought that he was with them constantly, joining them in all their activities, laughing at their jokes, comforting them when discouraged, constantly assuring them that one day soon they would all live together in untroubled serenity, speaking even of the excitement with which his dog would greet them.

One afternoon I was seated near the lake when the father asked if he could join me. He seemed to have nothing particular on his mind but was drawn as I was by the cheering energy of a beachful of children. There was, however, something on *my* mind.

"Are you not afraid to die?" I asked him.

"Of course, a little," he responded with a soft laugh. I don't know if it was the question or the tone in which I asked it that amused him, but he took it seriously in his gentle way.

"I'll tell you how I think of it," he said. "Notice how each child, coming to the end of the board, particularly if it is their first time in the water for the day, hesitates. The child has gone off that board scores of times, but he hesitates. He knows nothing will happen, but he pauses. There is still something that holds him back. But then he goes, and is back up on the board as quick as he can get there, and this time he goes right off." He turned to me. "You and I are first-timers. Neither of us, so far as we know, has ever been off the board before. We know nothing will happen—*of course* nothing will happen. But we hesitate."

"Yes, we do," I agreed. I realized that he had picked up my own uneasiness about death; indeed, what I was subconsciously expressing was a panic about having someday to stand at the end of the board. I suspect that part of my panic was not knowing whether I was standing there now.

But slowly the effect of his voice, and the certainty of his views, had an effect on my own feelings. I envied his lack of dread, and the untroubled face he turned toward me when saying what he said. Perhaps it was true, I found myself wishing.

Something gave me a start. I realized there was one fact about his son's death I did not know. "When did your son die?"

"Twenty-nine years ago in May," he answered in that same unperturbed style, his smiling eyes still focused on the activity at the diving board.

I am not sure what startled me, but I suspect it was the thought that all three of my own children were in the water before us, and I had been following their charged movements unaware. "Twenty-nine years," I said to myself, or maybe even aloud, stunned by the distance in space and time twenty-nine years would make in the relationships of my family. But this gentle man was not stunned, not at all, for the twenty-nine years he spoke of created no distances whatsoever. His son was as present to him as my nine year old daughter waiting in line for the diving board, hugging herself against the chill of a sudden breeze.

"Dad, look!" she cried, when she caught my attention. She flew off the end of the board and compressed her little body in a shape meant loosely to resemble a cannonball—and to cause an appropriate explosion in the water—but with as much success as could be expected of any skinny nine year old. If I had at that moment exclaimed to my friend that the shivering kid in the red-and-white suit was my daughter, I am sure that somewhere within his wounded heart he would also be pointing to a child—and smiling with pride.

These were people who had begged for more life, and in fact got it. They asked that death be taken away—and death was taken away. Death was now but one event in an unbroken cycle of events, and therefore no longer death. Death no more ended anything in their lives than a leap from the board ended the swimmers' play. Life and death had merged into a timeless whole that nothing could disturb.

"Dad, Dad! Watch this one!"

The child this man was watching had died when I was still a child, and would now be older than my own father. I could not help feeling that when these persons got what they asked for, it was not death that ended; it was their lives that had ended.

What I was aware of then was the awful isolation of this man and wife from the world around them. There was simply no way they could truly enter into the lives of any of these breathless cannonballers, for they could never be more than emblems for them—reminders. The reality of their lives would have to give way so that a little ghost and his dog could remain to comfort his parents. And, for the same reason, no one could enter into their lives. I could not know this old man where he lived; he could only *tell* me where he lived. There was no way I could really share his life with him. I could only look on with an indulgent smile. I sat next to him that afternoon but twenty-nine years away.

The reason I relate this experience is that, along with the kidnapped Italian general, it illustrates one aspect of the question of this meditation: How much life can we receive? The world brutally took away the life of this couple, and they reached out to get it back. But they made an elemental spiritual mistake: they wanted life without the world; they wanted life without pain or limitation. Once they had convinced themselves that they had never really lost their boy and his dog—and would one day be fully reunited—the real world ceased to compel their attention. Yes, they managed this rather well, but in an oddly dispassionate way, almost as though they had simply manipulated the controls of life that made it possible for it all to occur before them on a screen, while they sat back and waited. They have spent their lives waiting for life.

A genuine prayer for life is not a prayer for the end of death, but a prayer for the beginning of life. To receive life does not mean to receive a life that has no ending; it means to receive that which is always beginning. It means to receive that which has novelty in it, surprise, possibility, and, of course, pain. The biblical expression for such existence is "eternal life." We can be easily misled by this term into thinking that what is being offered is an unchanging status of some sort, a blissful terminus to all our journeying in which nothing new can ever happen again; indeed, in which nothing at all can happen. It is useful to recall that the great medieval mystic Meister Eckhart preferred the term "eternal birth" as a way of indicating the dynamic element in the life of prayer. Eternal birth is something of a contradiction, of course, for it is difficult to imagine being born over and over again through an eternity. One often suspects, however, that persons who enthusiastically claim to be "born again" mean to be born into a state in which they will hold out against all further change, as though to be born again is a specifiable condition in which one may remain forever. To be born again under these terms is more like dying than living. Eckhart instructs us that we are not to be born again, but to be born again, and again, and again, and . . .

If we think of life as eternal birth, and see birth as a radical beginning, we have put ourselves under the same risk as the *peregrini* who set to sea without knowing where they would be taken. To live as beginners is to be an expert at nothing, but to be awake to the unique details of our journey, taking all details as gift. However, if this is genuine risk then all that lies before us does not promise the happy outcome of the general, or the happy, disposition of that aged couple. Death lies out there among those possibilities, so does evil, and so do pain and disappointment and boredom. To receive life in the mode of eternal birth is to receive life that contains death.

The question for the kidnapped general is not whether God freed him from death, but whether God freed him for life. But this is everyone's question. We do not have to be seized by terrorists to know that we must beg for life. Whether we want to admit it or not, we have all been seized by terror, even if our lives have been outwardly free of danger or insecurity. The terror comes from our inner awareness that we cannot have life all by ourselves; that we depend on others to be at all, and especially others we cannot trust.

From a Christian point of view Socrates had it backwards. Philosophers, he said—and by philosophers he meant all thoughtful persons—live their lives training for death. It is as though they would learn in their meditations to walk to the end of the diving board without the least hesitation in mind or body, that they could dive as easily as they could take the next step. The parents of the boy and his dog were Socratics in precisely that sense. The reason that this is the obverse of faith is that Socrates, and those parents, did not in the end ask for anything at all. They wanted to be able to leap without risking anything, without leaving anything behind. It is as though they had walked to the edge of life, refusing to leave it until they could be sure that all they ever had they will be able to take with them. But the irony of this is clear: in trying to keep what they had, they have nothing.

My aged friends, and I think Socrates as well, wanted to live in their world without being limited by it. Death had occurred there, however, and changed it beyond repair. Instead of accepting that painful reordering of their lives, they chose to ignore the fact that death had happened at all. To do so has one obvious advantage: one can sustain a world that is always possible to live in. But it has one crippling disadvantage: it is a world no one else can live in.

It is precisely here that we can see why one of the difficulties of prayer is not that God gives us too little—but too much. To ask for life is not to get life without death; it is to get something far grander—life *and* death. Instead of regarding death as that which takes something away from us, we should regard death as that which has been given us, and therefore has the grace of the giver in it.

By contending that death has the grace of the giver within it, I do not mean to deny that we still die a most real death. Instead, I am suggesting that there is a decisive difference between receiving death and struggling against it. To receive death we must ask for it. Now I know how strange it seems to be urged to ask God for death along with life. But consider the consequence of praying that we be spared death. If we do not look on death as a gift, then we will see it as a loss, as something taken away from us. The term "loss" is important here. We can only lose that for which we are fighting, and we can fight only someone who is opposed to us. When death is understood as loss, it is as though life has been overcome by a superior opponent; we speak of the power of death, and mean by this something dark and malevolent. The inevitable effect of struggling against the power of death, which we can plainly see to be superior, is that we live as though life is already lost. Observe how often we hear the statement, "If death is the end, then why is life worth it?" Life appears vain, perhaps even shameful; we live as losers, angry and bitter over what little has been left us, and what little will remain.

The prayer for death is identical to the prayer for life. If death is given to us it ceases to be a malevolent opponent; and life ceases to be a struggle against it. Its shame drops away, along with its vanity. Each moment becomes precious, an occasion for joy. Instead of ruing how little is left us, we celebrate how much we have been given. We live neither as losers nor winners. We live as the recipients of a gift we most certainly could never have given ourselves.

The prayer against death is not therefore a prayer for life. To pray for unending life is, odd as it may seem, to close ourselves off as receivers of life. Like the old man and his wife we would live waiting to live, and in the meantime close the doors of our hearts to each other.

But we would also close ourselves against God. Consider the consequences of having an unending life—that no matter what happens we would continue to live. No matter what happens we would maintain the essential control over our lives, ultimately dependent on no one else. Immortality is a theatrical condition; it is having a thoroughly scripted life. But like life on the stage there is a lack of reality to it, a radical disengagement with those around us. If it does not ultimately matter to us what others do, then what does it matter to others what we do? We do not really talk with each other, but only recite our lines like so many soulless computers.

I mentioned before the common view that religious persons believe in immortality. This may be the case, but immortality is not, in fact, a *Christian* belief. In case this remark seems ill-informed let me prevail upon our stage theologian to address us on this point. It will be useful to learn from him that, although the theory of immortality slipped into Christian speculative thought in the early centuries, it is not a biblical teaching and can be supported by isolated quotations from the Bible only by dreadful forcing of the text. This theory has its origin in quite different soil, that of the Greek philosophers. I am sure our proper theologian would stress the fact that immortality is a state that cannot be reconciled with the biblical understanding of resurrection. For one thing, he would explain, resurrection is strictly an act of God. All references to it in the New Testament are in the passive mood: Jesus *was raised* from the dead, we *shall be raised* from the dead. It is a matter in which we are uncompromisingly dependent on God. For another, there is no saying exactly what we are raised into. If we were to satisfy ourselves with the Greek theory of immortality we may be certain, as was Socrates, that we continue being the persons we are. The Bible puts it differently. "Lo, we shall all be changed!" Paul declares. Ask him how and he must demur. "We see through a glass darkly." The theologian would not use our expression here, but we can see that he has just underlined the element of surprise in God's actions. There is something awaiting us we cannot foresee, or even understand. Risk again.

But there is more. The theologian concedes that the next

part is confusing, but insists that there are too many references on this point to be ignored: the Resurrection already has its effect on our lives. Eternal life is not something that waits for us on the other side of death; it is immediately available and has no essential relation to death. We are, of course, reminded of Eckhart's subtly paradoxical expression, eternal birth, and reflect for a moment on what it means to live as beginners. We can see that what the theologian is speaking about is what we have called a life of genuine listening in which every word we speak is an opening to another to say something previously impossible to say, thus giving our words a meaning we could not have thought them to have. He is telling us that the resurrection life is living not theatrically but dramatically. He does not, however, appeal to such terminology, but concludes his doctrinal apostrophe by quoting (again) Paul's exclamation, "Lo, I tell you a mystery. We shall all be changed."

How much life can we receive? The answer, as we now can expect, is paradoxical. If we do not pray for unending life, but pray for the life that has death in it, there is no limit to the amount of life we can receive. But in this case it is not a life that is exclusively our own, but a life that we have together. It is not a life without limitations—that is, a life without a world —but an intensely worldly life. Its worldliness, however, is a joyful worldliness, performed with celebratory enthusiasm, in recognition of the fact that the world as a whole is a gift freely given.

The question that opened this meditation had to do with God giving us far more than we ask for. How can we receive all that God has given us and remain within the limitations of our humanity? We are like the peasant girl in Kierkegaard's fable to whom the king can give absolutely everything—but not without profoundly confusing her, leading her to believe she is someone she is not. I divided that question into two parts, asking first how much life we can receive, answering that there is no limit to what we can receive. Now the second part of that question: How is it possible to live as the receivers of this unlimited gift? How can we live as the peasants we are and still be the receivers of our world?

I believe that the key here is to maintain a clear view of the fact that the world is something we *receive*, and not something we *have*. The dangerous error that confronts us here is that we will begin to think of ourselves as the possessors of a world, or to think of the world, in part or in whole, as our property, as though God has given us the world to do with as we like. One of the Bible's mightiest themes is that God is the creator of the world, the free giver of this most immense of gifts, but I am sure that the inner meaning of that teaching is not that God made a world for us to have, but a world for us to receive. What then is the difference between having and receiving?

Consider first the nature of having. It is meaningless to say I have anything unless I can dispose of it entirely as I wish, and only as I wish. If I have a dollar I can do with all one hundred cents of it whatever I wish without the least interference from anyone else. It happens at present to be the case, however, that everytime I spend a dollar the government requires that I pay eight cents of it in taxes. To say that the government *requires* me to do this implies that I do not spontaneously choose to pay these eight cents myself. I do not want to pay them. Now, it is true that the government does not absolutely *force* me to pay these taxes. I could most certainly refuse, but the price for doing so might be high. I might have to go hungry, or go naked, or go to prison. On its side the government has more than threats to offer me. If we all refused to pay our taxes we would have to do without fire and police protection, public transportation would come to a halt, and the water pipes would be shut off. We do not want to pay taxes, but we want these deprivations less, so we give up eight cents, or even twenty or thirty cents, of our dollar.

The more accurate way to describe my relationship with the government is not to say that I am forced to pay taxes, but that the government *competes* with me for that money. Each party to this contest has ways of strengthening its strategic advantage against the other. When the government moves to ease the poverty of some of its citizens, I may object to the transfer of "my" money to those who do not work for it, and express my objection by initiating or joining a political movement in support of a candidate who promises an end to welfare cheating. This is as much as saying that I have what I have of my dollar because I have *won* it in a struggle with my government.

But how did I get that dollar to begin with? It is likely that I had to work for it, that is, remove it from another's possession by offering that person goods or services more desirable than the dollar. My employer did not want to give up the dollar, but I have found a way of successfully competing for it. Some of my colleagues have found considerably more powerful strategies, and have loosened many more dollars from this possessive employer than I have been able to win.

The point here is that I have what I have only because I was able to win it from others who did not wish to give up possession of it. I possessed my red Ford convertible with the white leather seats and white sidewalls only because many others wanted also to have it but could not since, at least for the time being, I was in a superior competitive position. I won a kind of contest with them. It is for this reason that we say one holds "title" to property—the property is a sign that its owner has triumphed over someone else in some kind of struggle. The nature of property is, in fact, often discussed under the theory of entitlement. I am entitled to have whatever I can successfully take from someone else in what both parties agree is a fair contest. Fair or not, it is still the case—and the crucial point for us—that *property is always held against others*.

It should therefore not be surprising, when it is put this way, that property is a continuing spiritual issue. It is not that the things of the earth are inherently corrupting, that we dirty ourselves with mere objects, but rather that whenever we claim to have these things we set ourselves over others. It is not *what* we own that divides us; it is rather that we choose to divide it among ourselves by way of ownership. Property is not the cause, but the result, of our strife. This is so strongly the case that it can even be said that whenever persons object to the inadequacy of their possessions — though this might concern receiving what they deserve for their labor, or even what they need for the merest maintenance of their human dignity — they have assumed divisiveness within their primary community, and have in fact reinforced it. All questions of the distribution of property arise from rancor, and can only lead to more rancor, simply because opposition is inherent in the fact of property itself.

Christians must concede that their resolution of the problem of property has been notoriously unsuccessful over the centuries. They might be justified to some extent by the extreme form in which the spiritual issue in property is to be addressed. This is one matter on which the teachings of Jesus are quite unambiguous. Whatever Caesar claims is his, let him have; so too with God. Let each do what he or she wishes with their possessions. This effectively removes the question of ownership — as such — and focuses on another question: What do Caesar and God wish to do with what they have? The differences are clear: Caesar can only create his world by taking it away from us; God can create a world only by giving it to us. The grandeur of Caesar's world depends on how much he can win in his struggle with us; the grandeur of God's world depends on how much we are able to receive.

If having is always having something against each other, how is receiving different?

The first important difference concerns the *source* of whatever it is I possess or receive. As for what I possess, it is finally I who must be its source. That is, my possession of it must be the result of my own labor, or skill, or sacrifice. If it sounds a bit awkward to speak of being the source of one's own property, consider how this view is hallowed by such prosy wisdom as that found in expressions like, "only those who work deserve the bread," or, "money does not grow on trees." The implication is that you can claim possession to what you have only by the honest labor that went into obtaining it. True, your garden may have no money trees in it, but oranges and walnuts may be there aplenty. However, it is not by remaining on the trees that the fruit and nuts become yours. They do not become your property, as such, until you have—to borrow Locke's famous phrase—"mixed your labor with them." What comes to you unmixed with your labor never quite becomes yours; we will find something illicit and undeserved about it, and you may have to give it up to the authorities, or to the tax collector.

When we speak of receiving, on the other hand, it is evident that I cannot be the source of that which is given me. In fact, I cannot be the source of it in any sense whatsoever. Even if someone gives me a gift because I make them happy, it is not truly a gift but a kind of payment that I have earned. It is a gift I have won from them. Certainly, a great deal of our giving falls into this category. Our gifts are often a response to the gratitude we feel for the actions of another, or to the delight we take in the presence of another. In true giving there can be no *because*, no need or reason in the recipient for the gift.

This is why receivers can never anticipate what is to be given; indeed, a true receiver would not attempt to anticipate either what, or if, anything will be given. To live as receivers, therefore, is to live in the mode of surprise. It is to have an eye for novelty, for the sudden appearance of possibilities that could not have been imagined, much less planned for. To make the same point in the terms of biblical thinking, I am now speaking of what is to be considered in the biblical narrative revelation, or epiphany—those sudden disclosures in which we discover that God is offering something completely unanticipated. The gospels themselves are, in fact, set entirely in the mode of astonishment, suggesting even by the term "gospel" itself that the story told there is good news that could not have been anticipated. Though this is the case throughout the entire narrative of the life and ministry of Jesus, it is most vivid in both the birth and resurrection accounts. Great attention is given to the various announcements of the birth of Jesus, striking both joy and terror in the hearts of listeners, for there is a presentiment of great changes ahead, the appearance of possibilities that cannot be foreseen. Astonishment is also the prevailing atmosphere for each of the resurrection episodes, with the same mixture of dread and hope. The lengths to which the gospel writers have gone in finding intimations of these events in the Hebrew scriptures only has the effect of underscoring their historical uniqueness. The gospels are, in other words, highly dramatic documents over which the writers have occasionally attempted to throw a familiar script.

To live in the mode of surprise as a genuine receiver is not, however, as it may seem from these latter remarks, to live in a world of radical discontinuity. As astounded as Mary and the shepherds are, as startled as the women before the empty tomb or the disciples looking up from dinner at their risen Lord, they all learn in time that what has happened is not merely novel. What surprises them is that they can see for the first time that they are involved in a deeper and more consequent drama than they could possibly have imagined. Suddenly their lives have come to have a new meaning altogether.

To live as a receiver is, in other words, not only to live toward an open future prepared for surprise and unable to anticipate what is given; it is also to live with the expectation that the life that has already been lived will have an increasingly deeper and richer meaning. We discover with each gift, with each revelation, that we are more deeply connected with other people than we ever realized—and not only the persons involved with us now, but also those who have long since died and those yet to be born. Even our personal past wears a different face as we look back on it, for it is now more full of promise than we ever suspected at the time.

So far I have been discussing only what is implied in the fact that what the receiver receives has its source outside oneself, in another person. *But what is it that a giver gives*? When we live as receivers, *what* do we receive? I have already tried to make it clear that what we receive is life, but life with all the limitations and all the possibilities of a world. But in what form do we receive life? This question rises because of the temptation to think that life might be given as a kind of property. What has been said should make it clear that what the giver gives cannot in any sense be property.

It might be useful to pause here to consider more precisely why it is that we cannot give each other property. If we take seriously the fact that property is always held against someone—that is, it is property only because others would like to have it but cannot—then the giver of property only enters into a kind of collusion with the recipient, strengthening the latter's competitive status, raising the envy of others to whom the gift is given. This is such a common kind of giving that examples of it abound. The form with which I am presently most familiar concerns the education of children. Just a moment ago I stopped to do a little calculating and quickly discovered that there has been nothing in my lifetime, and quite likely will be nothing, on which I have spent more of my property than on the education of myself, my wife, and my three children. I now have to face a hard question. What was I giving when I paid for all of this with such a feeling of generosity? (Even when it felt like a sacrifice, I was still pleased with my magnanimity.) Was I doing all this toward the end of filling lives with surprise and awakening them to the deeper narrative of the race? Or was I hoping they would acquire the skills and personal associations that would promise a more propertied future? Was I, in short, in collusion with them against the others with whom they share their world?

There is no question in my mind but that when my brother and I were given that red Ford convertible we received it as property, as an object of envy that would significantly advance our various competitive activities. I was certainly aware that it was a sacrifice for my father, though now I have a more acute sense of the financial hardship this represented. Expressions of gratitude came easily and often from both of us for our father, but for all that I interpreted his generosity as a kind of conspiracy with his sons to act against the world.

What I discovered at the end of that summer was that he did not make the gift for the reason I thought he had. "I gave you this so you would never want it again." Just that simple sentence, and nothing more. Not one word passed between us again on this matter. If I was surprised to come home to that automobile, I was much more surprised by this statement. I knew at once that the astonishment came from what it revealed—about my father, about me, about life. It revealed a great deal more than I even wanted to know, and than I still want to know. He might just as well have said, "Yes, I gave you this car. But do you know whom it belongs to? It belongs to Caesar. So let him have it."

I learned that my father, in making this gift, did not care to compete with Caesar. This was not true of his life in general, however. I thought he spent a great deal of frantic energy trying to be Caesar, somehow trying to have it all. He quite obviously understood "having" to be synonymous with "taking," and engaged the world about him with a furious competitiveness, urging the same spirit on his children. I always understood these considerable efforts, almost always unsuccessful, to be inseparable from his expansive generosity. That is, he did not want to take his property from the world for himself; he took little apparent pleasure in his possessions. He did it for us. He thought if he were Caesar he could give us the world. But in this one brilliant moment, waiting for the traffic light to change, he set that pointless struggle aside. In fact, he set a great deal of himself aside. The Caesar in him went silent, and he listened. What he revealed in that simple sentence is that he had listened to what my brother and I were really saying—that we wanted something we could never truly have; that is, what we wanted was not the car, or what the car could bring us, but the wanting itself.

Of course, it is possible that my father could have put this same point quite directly. When we got home from the restaurant where we first saw the car, he could have sat back and explained to us that all we really wanted was the wanting, and that we had therefore set ourselves on a contradictory path. But had he done so it would have been with the voice of Caesar. It would have been a truth, a kind of theological pronouncement about the nature of things to which we were to listen in silent obedience. What is more, it would have been uttered as a judgment on our intentions, an assessment of the degree to which our lives had not taken the shape he desired. Most importantly, it would have been a pronouncement that cost Caesar himself nothing to say beyond the effort of saying it.

Instead, he cashed in his war bonds, emptied his checking account, drew all of his savings, borrowed money on the house and from friends, and did so with such an untroubled spirit that no sign of heroic sacrifice was anywhere visible. Because of his inherent generosity we were all given many beautiful and valuable things, but none of them had the astonishing revelatory power of this act, and the several others like it I can now recall. The reason is clear. What he gave us in this instance was not property, it was not the car; what he gave us was himself.

What do we receive from the giver? Not property, for since property always exists in the form of taking from others, it can neither be given nor be received. Though Caesar be in possession of the entire civilized world, he can give nothing and remain Caesar. What we receive from the giver is nothing less than the giver. Caesar is always free to give himself, but to do so he must first renounce his claim to Rome.

This is how Kierkegaard's fairy tale king resolves his dilemma. He does not give the world to his beloved, but gives up all claim to the world himself, empties himself of his royal prerogatives, takes on the life of a peasant, and gives himself to the girl. It is a perfectly dramatic act which leaves the future utterly open. Not once, Kierkegaard says, does the king appeal to a theatrical strategy by pulling back his peasant's garments to show the purple cloak beneath; not once does he resume the role of the king to shape affairs according to his desires.

Kierkegaard naturally meant his fairy tale to be taken as an analogy to the incarnation in which God sets aside all aspects of divinity to take on the life of a servant. It is characteristic of servants that they have placed their lives at the disposal of others; they have offered themselves as the most attentive of listeners. But the servant in this case brings us no objects whatsoever, giving nothing but himself. We can receive him only as he presents himself—in the silence of expectation, listening to our hearts. To receive him is therefore to take him into the heart. But now when we turn to the world with the Lord in our heart it is not to speak with the all powerful words of God, but to listen with the infinite patience of the silence of God.

Receiving the giver is not, therefore, a passive transaction like coming into the possession of property. It always means an active transformation of the receiver; it is always the beginning of something we cannot bring to an end. I have received nothing from my father if his giving has had no transforming effect on the way I live with others. If his remarkable listening to my contradicted heart on that one brief occasion does not allow me to listen to my own children, or to my wife, or a friend, or a student, or a stranger, I have not lived as the receiver of his gift. My father has been dead many years, but I have not finished receiving what he gave me—and continues to give. Death, you can see, had no effect on that gift. If anything stops his giving it is not the silence of his death but the noise of my life. It is my resistance to putting out in the small rudderless boat that true listening requires. It is my preference for the role of professorial Caesar, holding title to an empire of coveted knowledge.

As you see, these meditations have not been concerned with the techniques of praying, and do not offer samples of prayers appropriate for special circumstances. I do not imply by this omission that such matters are irrelevant. It is rather that material of the highest quality is already available on this subject. My task has been to look at the nature of prayer itself. If you can accept the view that prayer is an asking of the heart and a corresponding receptiveness, you will probably also see that the matter of technique, the *how-to* of praying, wears an altered appearance. If one prays from the heart almost any technique will do. Say your prayers in Edwardian English, or Latin, or Hebrew, or in tongues; say them in your car, in your neighborhood Methodist Church, in the frenzy of Spirit possession or the rapture of pentecostal abandon, say them in the cadenced decorum of the Book of Common Prayer; speak your heart to your lover, to your children, to your therapist, to total strangers—the simple point is that if you do speak from the heart, God listens. The silence of God is everywhere. There is no conceivable human setting in which God is not present, listening. No matter whether anyone else is listening.

I want to finish this last meditation here, but my invented theologian has been quietly importuning me for the past few moments. He has been urging me to return once more to the point he made earlier concerning prevenient grace. I know what he has in mind, and perhaps we should conclude with it, for it will require us to exit as we entered—by way of paradox.

Remember that the prevenience of grace means only that

God comes *before* us in every instance; God comes before all things. "In the beginning, God . ." are the first words of the Bible. However we may speak about it, it is always the case that God does not respond to us; we respond to God. God is already silent, and does not become silent when we speak. This has a very important application to prayer, and we can understand here why the theologian is insisting on having this last word. We do not get God's attention by speaking from the heart. Speaking from the heart is possible only because we already have God's attention.

One of the most common questions about prayer has to do with its efficacy: Does God actually answer when we call out our deepest inner longings? What our theologian wants us to see is that praying from the heart *is* God's answer. To speak from the heart is to ask and to receive at the same time. The *ask* and the *receive* are simultaneous and inseparable. Whomever you speak to from your heart you receive in your heart. Since you will always speak to God when you truly ask, you will have God in your heart—in the very act of asking. But at the same time you will receive all that God is giving you: life in all its joyful worldliness. Ask, then, for what you are already being so abundantly given.